WHO
CARES?

SIMPLE WAYS
YOU
CAN REACH OUT

WHO
CARES?

By Marcy Heidish

WHO CARES?
Simple Ways **YOU** *Can Reach Out*

Copyright © 1997 by Marcy Heidish

Printing History
First Printing, 1997, Ave Maria Press, Notre Dame, IN
ISBN 0-87793-599-8

Republication, 2009, Dolan & Associates, Publishers
ISBN-13: 978-0-9792404-6-1
ISBN-10: 0-9792404-6-8

LIBRARY OF CONGRESS CATALOGING-IN-PUBLICATION DATA

Heidish, Marcy.
    Who cares? : Simple Ways You Can Reach Out / Marcy
    Heidish.
    p. cm.
    ISBN 978-0-9831164-5-5
    Includes bibliographical references.
    I. Title.
Library of Congress Control Number: 2010942512
....
Third edition

For My Father

My deep gratitude
to these gifted practitioners of the art of caring:

• Sister Mary Ann Luby, G.N.S.H., who supervised my work in shelters for homeless women;

• the Rev. Keith Keidel, my supervisor in Clinical Pastoral Education at Sibley Memorial Hospital, Washington, DC;

• Father Michael Bryant, Head Chaplain at the District of Columbia Jail;

• and the late Father Thomas P. Gavigan, S.J., my beloved friend and mentor for twenty years.

• My thanks, without measure, for these great teachers as well:
  • my family of caring friends,
  • the women of the shelters,
  • the residents of the jail,
  • the people of several assisted care facilities,
  • the hospital patients and their families,
  • and my students at Georgetown University.

• I am also grateful for the outstanding editorial guidance I've received on ths book from Robert Hamma, an editor for all seasons.

CONTENTS

Prologue

You're on your way.

You know this path, you've walked it for awhile. Ahead, the road gibbons out, predictable and smooth. Still a lot of ground to cover. You quicken your step — and ahead, you see the wayfarer, stumbling on the edge of the road. You glimpse the leaning back, the mass of bundles. Can you pass? Or should you try to help? Unsure, you draw nearer.

Now, you see the bundles clearly: roped together, heavier than you thought. Nothing you can do.... You look away. You watch your step. Silence — then a muffled cry. Now, you're moving forward. Now, without quite knowing why, you fall into step with the wayfarer.

Slowly, the silence warms and chanes; together, you walk, you keep pace. Shouldering a bundle's edge, you can feel the weight lighten a little. In the wayfarer's face, for just a moment, you see others: family, friends, strangers... But now the road is steeper, and the wind's a keen blade, slicing sharp across your eyes. Into wind and grade, you lean together, and the sky flies by above you like a tattered banner, and you're telling stories, you and the wayfarer....

<1>

The Practice of Caring

*For I was hungry and you gave me food, I was
thirsty and you gave me something to drink, I was
a stranger and you welcomed me, I was naked and
you gave me clothing, I was sick and you took care
of me, I was in prison and you visited me.*
    — Matthew 25:35-36

This book is designed for the caring person within each
of us. We may be busy, we may be weary, but I don't
believe we have ceased to care about one another. In the
midst of life's demands, however, we may have lost touch
with this part of ourselves. And we may need to learn —

or relearn — some basics: the craft as well as the art of caring. These pages are meant to empower that caring self and equip it with specifics for practicing the art of caring, especially within your immediate circle of concern: family, friends, neighbors, and coworkers.

This book is meant to companion you as you begin — or begin again — to practice the art of caring. This can be an amazing journey: you don't end up where you start out. Each destination is a new path. The journey itself may be the destination. And on all such journeys of the spirit, it helps to have a guide. I hope this book may be that for you, whether you travel across town or across the street; across the office or across your own kitchen. Truly, tangibly, you can make a difference.

Familiar Words

- *"I've got it all — why do I feel something big is still missing?"*
- *"She's going through a rough time; I just don't know what to do."*
- *"I'd like to make a difference, somehow — more than this."*
- *"Somewhere over the rainbow, dreams come true. Then what?"*
- *"I feel stuck in my safe little space — anyone got a crowbar?"*

- *"My neighbor needs help; wish I knew where to start."*

- *"I really want to give something back ... but how?"*

As writer and friend, chaplain and teacher, counselor and seminarian, I have heard those words for years — once I started listening. In the rush and push of daily life, we may forget the power of the caring person within us. And then, almost imperceptibly, something makes us remember. Sometimes, it's a sense of being stuck, a sense of something missing in our lives. Sometimes, it's the desire "to make a difference" or "give something back." And other times, we simply have no choice. Sooner or later, we are faced with others in crisis, in pain, in difficulty, on rocky ground with a great deal to carry. How we do we respond to them? That may depend on the situation — and on us.

As a child, I went with my mother to a vast department store. We gazed at hundreds of coats that hung, it seemed, on the air itself. The hour was early, the place was still. And then, amidst this hush, I felt my mother stiffen. Not far away, a woman stood motionless. I'd seen her somewhere else: waiting for her son, outside our school. Now she seemed to wait for something else. Staring beyond the racks, she was tracing endless circles on a coat's fur collar.

Abruptly, my mother swept me out of the store, onto the street. In the morning light, I saw that her eyes were wet. It seemed a long time before she spoke: "Her husband lost his job. I didn't know what I should ... maybe she'd rather not talk ... then again, I wish..." Her words trailed off. I remember my mother's tears. I remember the woman among the coats, though I cannot recall her name.

Since then, from time to time, I've walked with wayfarers, by chance and by intention. And sometimes, of course, I have been the stumbler on the way, with unlaced shoes, untidy baggage. We have all plowed on, now and then, beneath our own snarled, weighty bundles. Perhaps we wanted to struggle alone, biting at the wind, gasping out "I can handle it," even as we fell and fell again. Perhaps we called for help and no one seemed to hear.

Maybe, though, someone fell into step with us. Funny how we never forget those who companion us, even briefly, on those journeys through the dark. It is good to recall those times, however we may prefer to forget them. If we claim those times, they can become sources of strength and insight. And they can help us walk with others on the path. These memories are essential "gear" to pack for the road ahead.

A New Term for Success

On my own journey, I have been blessed with extra-ordinary guides, good maps, and traveling companions who taught me more than I could have imagined. One of my mentors, Sr. Mary Ann Luby, directed Rachel's

Shelter for Homeless Women for a dozen years. I can see her still, in her faded jeans, telling me stories at the kitchen sink. "We need to redefine success," she said. "It isn't in having, but in being. My experience has been one of privilege — witnessing resurrection every day."

Whatever form it takes, wherever you are, that privilege waits for you.

For you, the art of caring may be the unspoken art — the one that lies half-hidden, waiting to be recognized, coaxed forth, empowered. In the other arts, we understand the need for inspiration, practice, craft — but we may not look at caring the same way. In fact, to state that within each of us, a caring person waits to act, is to state something quietly revolutionary. And I believe it is true.

I believe it, quite simply, because I have seen evidence; evidence so strong, so surprising, it defies even the most seasoned skepticism. I have seen it in classrooms and hospital rooms, nursing homes and funeral homes, in the office and in the neighborhood. And so have you: at home, at work, with friends, with strangers, in yourself.

I have also seen the caring person within remain just that — locked inside, unsure about the "basics" of this art: where to start, what to say, how to help in any number of daily situations. This book is designed to provide specific, basic tools for that inner caring self as it emerges, and also the inspiration to overcome the "Who me?" syndrome.

Who Cares?

We don't have to be saints to act on the caring impulse, to practice the art of caring. What we do need is the weave of inspiration and basic craft that undergird any art. We need some guidance; we need some practice. And the more we practice, the more we open our lives to flashes of glory in the ordinary, a Celtic concept. In those moments, even briefly, we transcend ourselves. We glimpse in ourselves more that we ever thought we could be. We glimpse, too, our deep connections with others, even in an era of disconnection.

I recall a man named Graham, a professional man, successful, who felt a core of emptiness in his life all the same. He knew, he said, that he wasn't what he could be, despite the diplomas on his walls. He wanted to make a difference, somehow, as a person, as Graham. After a while, he heard of a need for food and toiletries at a house in his neighborhood, a family with troubles. Never had he cooked or baked, but after some thought, Graham went into his kitchen. He opened some prize pecans: a gift from a friend in Georgia. He followed a recipe with care.

It was a Thursday when he carried his brownies to these scarcely known neighbors. A shy man, he had to overcome his reluctance to intrude. When invited in, he placed his baking on the strange kitchen table. Outside, he found himself speaking aloud: "Graham, you *finally* did something." He still brings his pecan brownies to the neighbors — five years later. Now, his presence is as happily anticipated as his baking. And he says he feels transformed.

This book is designed to facilitate such "everyday" transformations. It is my hope that these pages will inspire, guide, and provide specific steps in the art and practice of caring. I will draw on my confluence of experiences as writer and teacher, seminarian, chaplain and counselor — and as companion on the way.

The Challenge of Caring

This book will focus on the reader's immediate circle of concern: family, friends, neighbors, coworkers. We are constantly challenged in that seemingly ordinary arena.

Sooner or later, we are all faced with someone in difficult times, someone whose troubles brush our lives. So often, we feel unsure about our response. What to do — and how? What to say — how to act? What is enough? Too much? Too little? Those questions, left unanswered, tend to paralyze us. But must they? Must *we* settle for "if only's" and "should have's"?

It is my hope that this book will offer alternatives to these blocks, partly through inspiration, partly through "basic craft." Each chapter will include wise, illuminating quotes for reflection. I see the reader as participant.

You Care

I believe this is "a book for all seasons," directed at a multi-faceted readership. I think it is important to address this diverse readership now. I do not see this as a "religious" or sectarian book; nor do I see it as a book for "caregivers" per se, a term which often denotes specialized "helping professions" — clergy and lay leaders, those who care for the chronically ill, emotionally troubled, people in crisis, etc. I note in many ordinary people signs of rising interest in enacted, everyday caring, and I am convinced that there is a far wider audience for this book, including....

Baby Boomers: They are the largest segment of the book-reading community. Boomers are reaching the life-stage of "arrival." They have met, or are meeting, their primary goals. But many say that something still seems to be missing. "I have it all," a fortyish lawyer told me.

"But still there's something missing. I'd like to give something back, make a difference in some other way."

Once primary goals are met, we may feel most keenly a need to make a difference — in a new way. In 1995, a series of *Washington Post* articles discussed this desire to make a difference, as well as the ways people acted on the impulse. Many Baby Boomers who read these articles told me that the subject was catalyzing.

Generation X: This book is also intended for people in their twenties — the so-called Generation X. Many in this age group (whom I have taught) resent stereotypes of indifference and non-caring. This readership also wants to act on the caring impulse. In January 1995, *Mademoiselle* magazine ran an article on how to help a friend in crisis. Two years ago, *Glamour* magazine ran a piece on the popular slogan, "Practice random acts of kindness.

Those Who Form Values: Clergy and parish lay leaders, parents and teachers all have a special role in forming values in young people. This book is for them and for everyone who wishes to call forth the caring person within. That person deserves recognition and reinforcement. This can happen through inspiration, but this must be translated into everyday life. Step- by-step practice in the craft and practice of caring, in turn, enable the art.

Empowering Those You serve

In my six published novels, I have usually written about characters who model the art of caring. In the novel *A Woman Called Moses* (made into a TV movie with Cicely Tyson), I focused on Harriet Tubman, conductor on the Underground Railroad and, as such, one of the most original hands-on practitioners of the caring arts. So, too, with Mother Elizabeth Seton, the first American-born saint and the heroine of my novel, *Miracles*.

In this book, I draw from my studies in the Washington, D.C. Consortium of Seminaries where my area of special interest was pastoral care. My greatest teachers and classrooms, however, were in the hospital and jail where I served as an assistant chaplain, and in the nursing homes and homeless shelters where I volunteered regularly for six years. In my parish I have also trained volunteers in various forms of pastoral care. Through these pages, I hope to share what all these experiences taught me.

Since 1990, I have taught at George Washington University, Howard University, and Georgetown University's School of Summer and Continuing Education. My students have taught me a great deal, and I have watched with joy as they have empowered each other. *Who Cares?* is designed to guide and teach and empower *you* and those you may be teaching.

Everyday Action

Everywhere, I have listened to people speaking of a need to "make a difference," "to connect on another level," "to give something back," and "to know what to say, what to do when someone's having a rough time ... when bad things happen." It is my hope that this book will meet those needs and desires, that it will be a book grounded in experience, illuminating to the spirit, and precise in step-by-step guidance. I believe that the caring impulse can be translated into everyday action. May these pages guide and companion you in the art of caring.

■

<2>

The Receivers of Caring

There's been a Death in the Opposite House
As lately as Today
I know it by the numb look
Such Houses have — alway —
        — Emily Dickinson

Sooner or later, we will all see that sight, even if it is not precisely that way. We may hear of a death or illness in our apartment building, in our neighborhood, our parish, or perhaps a car pool community.

And how do we respond in a caring way?

"I just don't know how to keep going. I come here to work everyday, I try to do my job, but each day it's harder. I'm afraid to tell anyone else...." Over a casual work day lunch, between bites of turkey on rye, you get a taste of a colleague's deepening depression. You swallow hard. You study the face across the table. You have noticed your coworker's usual humor had been muted these last few months, but frankly you had no idea that there was anything seriously wrong. Sooner or later, you will confront a similar issue — some difficulty in a colleague's life, which presents you with a choice and that same question:

How do you respond in a caring way?

The call comes late at night. For a moment you don't recognize the voice — the voice, you suddenly realize, of a long-time friend. "I can't believe it." The voice trembles on the other end of the line. "I left him tonight, but I've been leaving, I guess, for years. I know you must be shocked. I don't know what will happen. Please understand...."

And sooner or later, this too will happen, the voice of a friend wavering to you across a phone line, the night air, or the space between your chair and hers; a voice that tells you of a major life upheaval, a secret grief, an abiding struggle. And once again, in a different way, you will ask yourself the same question:

How do I respond in a caring way?

As we reflect on the challenge of caring, we come to recognize that preparation, forethought, and reflection enable us to respond to each different situation in an appropriate way. If we are more intentional, as well as reflective and prayerful, about our caring response, we can adjust for each new situation in the most creative, giving manner. That response can take many forms, depending on where we stand in relation to the other.

Regardless of the kind of relationship we have with the troubled person, there are certain undergirding conditions and questions which remain the same:

- *Should I intervene or respect the person's privacy?*
- *If I intervene, how should I approach the situation?*
- *What special gifts can I bring?*
- *What special weaknesses in me should I watch for?*
- *How can I simply be present in this situation?*

It may be helpful to keep a checklist like the one above. Perhaps you bring a variety of gifts, from being a good listener to your own experience, to a knowledge or interest, for example, in poetry or baseball, which may be shared.

Perhaps you know your own weaknesses, as well. A tendency to judge too quickly, a tendency to get too involved or become too detached. Perhaps you have been raised to respect others' "privacy" as a kind of social code, or as a way to avoid involvement and intimacy.

Or, perhaps, you have always found yourself managing people's affairs, and have been surprised and hurt when they mysteriously resent it. Maybe you have never approached anyone in trouble because you simply don't know what to do, what to say, as we discussed in another chapter.

Let us first address that most pressing and primary challenge. To become involved or not ... and, if so, how. Each response will vary, as we have said, depending on where you stand in relation to the person and on the ring of the relational circle.

The first action is an internal one, I believe. We must reflect carefully: Am I called to this? Is this where God wants me to be?

Deepening Discernment

Do not listen only to the top layer of your discernment process — the layer which will feed back to you fear, dread, perhaps a desire to flee. As St. Ignatius suggests in his writings on discernment, it is important to listen to undercurrents of a sense of rightness and peace, even if these move like tides under surface waves on an ocean.

You may not have time to do extensive prayer-work and reflection *immediately*. But this process should undergird your entire caring journey so that you feel companioned as you companion others. Even if we cannot take a long time to do a complex visualization, when the phone rings, when the news comes, when the ambulance arrives across the street, we may cultivate the habit that St. Teresa of Avila calls "Arrow Prayer." This is, a brief, focused moment of prayer. And it is, I believe, a habit that can be developed, practiced, and built into our routine way of handling things.

After you have made your discernment, you may want to ask for confirmation in prayer — or you may feel resolved and right about proceeding. After you practice this process, you will become more adept at sensing your "inscape," a term used by the great poet-priest Gerard Manley Hopkins to refer to one's own inner landscape, its "weather systems" and rhythms, and God's movement throughout it. This is a lifelong process, one in which you need to be patient and gentle with yourself.

Suppose now you feel called to approach a person in difficulty or to get involved to some degree. Whether the person is a neighbor or coworker, your approach will be shaped by the person's expression of need. There may be no expression at all: no cry for help, no confided secret — perhaps only something like the "house across the way" in Emily Dickinson's poem.

There may be, however, a veiled call for help: a repeated invitation to lunch, a shared confidence, "acting out" through some form of inappropriate behavior. This behavior may be a coworker missing a series of deadlines, almost, it seems, on purpose; or it may be an outburst or a startling absence for some event. Or there may be a direct plea, though in my experience this is more rare and less problematic.

A Circle of Concern

Think about your family, friends, neighbors, and co-workers. You may see them in a formation resembling a series of concentric circles. There is that inner circle: those most intimate people in whom you confide and for whom you would be there, even in the middle of the night. Then there is another ring, comprised of people who are important to you — and to whom you are important — but this circle is somewhat less intimate. You care about one another but you may not confide quite so much; there may be somewhat less frequent contact. Then there are outer circles of friends, neighbors, and coworkers, all the way to the outermost ring I would term "friendly acquaintances."

In this book, I see friends and neighbors as one multi-dimensional group. We all have friends who are geographically neighbors as well. We also have friends who may live at a distance, but who through the power of spiritual connections — not to mention the phone, fax, and mails — are "neighbors of the heart," nonetheless. This is certainly true for me with friends and prayer partners as far away as Idaho and Mississippi.

There are also other areas in which friends, neighbors, and coworkers overlap. Look at your own landscape and you will see this is true; so often, artificial distinctions blur. We all have friends, neighbors, colleagues on different levels.

It may be useful for you to draw concentric circles on a pad of paper and see whom you place in your concentric rings. It may also be interesting to draw another series of concentric circles and date it back five years. You may notice changes, a natural part of the dance of life. You may notice something else: the level of intimacy, in my experience, does not always seem dependent on the length of an association.

For example, friends, neighbors, or coworkers of twenty years may have moved on, or some of your bonds with them may have shifted through time. On the other hand, "old" ties may still form your inner circle. I have several friends of three to five years' standing who were instantly kindred spirits and remain in my inner circle. I believe they always will.

I recall the blessed friendship that I formed with my first editor, Anne Barrett. She was in her early seventies, I in my twenties. In a very short period, we became as close as could be; that chemistry, that communion between souls, was just "there."

I remember sitting with Anne before her hearth, unlit. We drank tea, we talked and talked, we read to each other until we noticed we could no longer see the print on the page. Dusk had fallen around us and we, so absorbed in conversation, had forgotten to turn on any lights. I guess we had our own.

Anne said to me once, "At my age, I didn't expect to begin a new friendship — especially one that goes deep." I think, for me, it is inner depth rather than chronological length that determines with whom I feel the closest —

and this intimacy transcends such labels as "friends," "neighbors," and "coworkers."

Using the model of concentric circles, you may ask, "Is it easier to express caring for those on the inner than outer rings?" I believe this varies. Sometimes we fear intruding on those with whom we feel the least intimate — those on the "outer rings." On the other hand, sometimes it is easier to reach out to this ring because we bring less emotional baggage with us. With our most intimate relationships, it may be easier to express caring and this expression may seem more natural. However, we carry much more emotional freight on this level, and we still need to be careful about trespassing on private areas, even in our closest associations.

Caring in Your Family

Let us consider first the area of family. So often I have heard clergy, social workers, counselors, and physicians say it is most difficult to minister to family. It is sometimes harder to be objective, patient, and to remember whatever pastoral instruction we have received. Again, this is because such situations are so emotionally charged. I see this in my own life as I relate to my mother who has become chronically ill. With all my training in chaplaincy, pastoral care, and counseling, I find it harder to care for my mother, perhaps because I care so very intimately. However, if I allow myself to stop, pray, and think before I react, I find I can be more helpful.

Our earliest models of caring come from our families. Naturally, these affect us as adults. For example, my father was a dedicated surgeon. From the time I can remember, the phone would ring in the middle of the night and I would hear my father take his "black bag" and go out. He made house calls long after that practice nearly disappeared. And he made them in a vast metropolitan area. He often treated the poor and elderly for no cost, people who paid him "in kind" — meat from a butcher, repair work from an electrician, homemade cookies from a widow. Without realizing it, my father modeled for me what it means to care, although in this case, the modeling was done in a professional context. We can all remember negative modeling as well, within our own family circle. And we may react to this reality in several ways. One way is to repeat the negative behavior and "look out for number one" to the exclusion of others. Another way is to react against that modeling by consciously deciding to model the *reverse of* the negative behavior.

Again I offer an example from my own life. My father, so generous to his patients and often to his family, was a child of the Great Depression. In restaurants, when we went out to dinner, he would forbid my mother and me to order anything except a main course — no salad, no dessert, etc. A quirk, perhaps, but one that created great tension. I remember deciding when I was about ten, as I sat at one of those silent dinners, that I would never be like that. For what it's worth, I never have been. And so I learned both negative and positive role modeling from my father. Perhaps you have, too — from your parents and others in your family system. There are other role models, of course, in our formative early years: teachers, clergy, counselors, etc. They all shape us in some way.

As we grow up and form new family systems, we may need to balance the art of caring with our families' needs and with our family commitments. Sometimes a family member may feel hurt or rejected if we spend the evening with a sick neighbor instead of at home, at dinner, helping with homework, or "just killing time," as a spouse put it to a clergy friend. How do we handle the tension that sometimes exists between commitment to family and commitment to caring beyond the family circle?

Sometimes we must make a choice based on urgency of need. But if we wish to build the art of caring into our lives, long-term, we need to explain to our families why this is important to us. Such an explanation is most helpful when it turns into a discussion, where everyone can express feelings. It is crucial for us to make clear in action, as well as words, that the family is not being put on the "back burner," or rejected.

One very helpful way to demonstrate this is to invite family participation in your caring activities. I know of spouses, at first reluctant, who came along to visit sick neighbors or troubled friends and eventually began to develop ministries of their own. I have also seen the powerful effect on children who accompany parents to hospitals, nursing homes, and homeless shelters. These visits not only include the whole family, but, again, provide important role modeling and inspiration.

Caring with Friends

Friendship is unique as a caring relationship which is created, not inherited. As an only child, I know this first hand. As an adult, I have found the sisters and brothers I never had in my precious friends.

Friendship requires "gardening." This gardening or nurturing of the relationship can be a great joy, and as with all gardens, requires steady commitment. One way we can be good gardeners and stewards of friendship is to follow the suggestions made above about family. Friends may feel some of the same hurt and rejection as families when we enact the art of caring in wider circles. And so it is equally important to explain the art of caring to our friends, inviting discussion and offering assurance of the friendship's importance. Perhaps — if the person so desires — you can include your friend in your caring activities. The art of friendship helps us with the art of caring. Friendship is a great teacher in caring for family and ourselves, and it strengthens us to reach out to others.

For example, a woman I know who began to practice the art of caring in a more intentional way said she draws on experiences as a friend and translates them to new caring situations. She has accompanied ill friends to the doctor. She thinks what she talked about and how she was with her friend at the doctor as she accompanies someone in need of support to an AA meeting.

While this book will focus most directly on the art of caring for neighbors and coworkers, one step beyond the traditional nuclear family, it is my hope that these pages will be of some help in caring for both the members of your family as well as the stranger on the rim of the circle. Each of these subjects could well be a book unto itself.

The rest of this chapter concerns itself with two circles in your immediate world: neighbors and co-workers. In each circle, we may be challenged to practice the art of caring, and each circle presents certain similarities and certain differences, as does each individual situation. We will see what they have in common and how they are different, and we will learn how flexible is the art of caring so that it may encompass them all, and others as well.

Practicing the Art of Caring: Neighbors

Across the street from my friend, Jo, in a suburban area, near a big city, a couple had lived for a long time. Jo did not know them, although she occasionally exchanged a wave with the wife when they were both going to their cars. Jo did know that the husband was chronically ill with cancer, was effectively cared for at home, and that his wife was his primary caregiver. The situation had been going on for so long that no one thought much about it; it seemed as if the neighbor's cancer was an ongoing and non-acute condition.

The couple did not socialize with anyone on the block and yet they were not a forbidding, alienating presence. They simply went about their business while their neighbors went about theirs. Jo had often wondered if perhaps she should knock on their door sometime — to do what? Just say hello? Introduce herself? Ask how things were going? Ask if she could be of help? Somehow she had never done this; on what pretext would she go? A holiday, perhaps? Was a pretext necessary? Would she be intruding? Perhaps, she told herself, yet that nagging "what if" remained.

About a year ago, Jo returned from om work to see an ambulance in front of the neighbors' house. Stricken, Jo's hand fluttered to her mouth. The husband must have died. Both her hands rose to cover her face when she discovered that it was the wife, instead, who had died of a heart attack. Now Jo's "what if's" turned to "if only's." She wished she had not waited for a pretext, that she had not put off her visit. The neighboring wife had looked so cheerful, so capable, that Jo never thought she, needed help.

But upon reflection, Jo realized that, of course, anyone in a chronic care situation would need help. Jo could not know for sure how wide this neighbor's support network was, if she did not ask. Even now, the memory of this incident is painful for Jo, and it is one she relives, playing out various scenarios every time. What should she have done, Jo asked me.

It's my sense that there are no "should's," but there are always possibilities. Jo had felt some sense of calling to make contact with the neighbor, but had been "hobbled," in Jo's words, by a stronger sense of helplessness — uncertainty about how, when, what to say or do. I believe that we have all found ourselves in this dilemma, and when a similar incident confronts us, I think its power can be used to inform the next opportunity. We can turn our regrets and "if only's" into focused, motivated energy. It is also important to recognize the fear of the "nosy neighbor" role..

There are times when we have been in pain, or difficulty, and have decidedly *not* wanted anyone to get too close; those moments of self-protection must be respected. However, I feel that it is even more important, and certainly just as respectful, for the person. in difficulty to be given an option — the chance to accept help.

Perhaps Jo might have gone across the street and left a note with a small bouquet of flowers. The note might have read something like this: "Just to let you know that I think of you and hope you'll call on me if you ever need a hand ... (or) If you might like to join me for a cup of tea at my place ... (or) I'm going to the store and wondered if you'd like me to pick anything up while I'm there."

The advantage of a note is this: it doesn't put the recipient on the spot or seem to demand an instant response. It does, however, convey a sense of caring, and at the same time gives the neighbor a chance to say no, if the invitation comes at a bad time or seems an intrusion.

I think the reinforcement of one's caring presence is also important. The person in difficulty may feel shy about responding the first time, but the next time (perhaps a week or two later) the note-sender's sincerity is repeated is another opportunity to respond. If you have a "waving acquaintance" with a neighbor, crossing the street or hall and speaking briefly may be more congruent with the relationship.

I recall establishing a friendship with a very isolated person on my street through two notes and a book on cats. This neighbor used to walk up the street in the twilight with her four cats in parade behind her. As a cat-owner and lover, myself, I let my neighbor know, quite genuinely, how much I appreciated the sight of her with her feline procession.

At the time of the first note, however, I must admit that I felt foolish and tentative; I really didn't expect a response. I don't know what gave me the courage to leave the note in the neighbor's door: some strong sense of loneliness and isolation surrounding this person as she walked, and some perception of a silent cry for someone, anyone, to care. I wondered, at first, if I was being fanciful. To my astonishment, I learned from this neighbor that she was indeed wondering if it mattered to anyone if she lived or died.

I am hardly possessed of any special perceptions, but I think we all have a great deal of intuition if we pay it heed. We can pick up much about body language, facial expressions, tones of voice, if we get in the habit of *really* observing, *really* listening (without making the other person feel like he or she is under a microscope).

Another situation touches this neighboring of our immediate circle, but in a different way. The above "givens" were these: I didn't know the person except to wave to, say hello to, but something seemed wrong and I wanted to *make myself available and give the person the option of a caring presence.* But what if you know the person in that "middle-distance" way, where you do stop to chat about snow or raking leaves or the like, but do not have a close, personal relationship with your neighbor?

I was thrown into such a situation before I had begun my own reflections on the intentional art of caring. It was a chilly autumn night about four years ago, a Sunday night of swirling leaves, when everyone on my street was snug at home. An ambulance appeared in front of the house to my left, where there lived a recent widower, in his seventies and in what seemed the prime of good health. He played golf, clipped all of our edges, and often kindly raked leaves off common walkways without being asked. His grown daughter had moved to another part of the county with her husband, but was often around. He also had a serious new romantic relationship with a woman who was, that night, on her farm about an hour away. The street was so quiet; the ambulance's siren was shrill, startling, as were the flashing lights. A team of paramedics rushed into the house.

I don't know why I went outside; I grew up in Manhattan, in a large apartment building where it was considered bad form to go beyond polite greetings to neighbors. But I did go outside, because I was fond of this man I did not know well, because of his never failing cheer, the warmth of his smile, the willingness to be a good neighbor, but not an intrusive one. I knew on an intuitive level that in some way I was a daughter-figure for him. I remembered dozens of conversations about nothing special as I went to my car and he paused as he mowed grass. Nothing special, and, yet, somehow, very special. There was an unspoken connection between us.

And so I went outside and stood at the foot of the path to his front door, and after awhile other neighbors joined me. A handful of us stood in the chilly night while the paramedics and the neighbor's daughter were visible, eerily illuminated by the overhead light in the living room and framed by the large picture window. We did not know if we should knock or not, and so we stayed, keeping the silent vigil. At some point, if we were needed, we knew we wanted to be available.

After awhile, a police car arrived and the ambulance left, without a passenger. We waited several minutes, guessing the worse. Again, we were not sure what role to play, but there was tacit agreement that we wanted to be there in case we could do something, in case someone called, and as a kind of honor guard for our neighbor. Finally, one of us who had known this family for a long time burst from our little group. As if she could not contain herself any longer, as if all her caring, worry, and fear, broke loose, she rushed up the path and entered the house.

We waited, We could see her comforting the weeping daughter in the window. Then, slowly, tentatively, one by one, many of us approached the house. Our neighbor had died of a heart attack during a nap. The familiar house was somehow changed.

I remember the daughter's tears wet my blouse as I hugged her in the kitchen. I had held my arms out to her, impulsively, and had not expected her response. A friendship formed out of that moment, though at the time all I knew was that it felt right and important to be there, to simply be there.

I think this incident illustrates many aspects of the art of caring. One, it seems to me a good and helpful thing to make oneself available, while giving the other person the ultimate choice as to whether our offer of presence will be taken. The other person retains his or her dignity and the right to say yes or no.

But if we do not make ourselves available, how can we know what is needed?

Further, we must let the other person know we are available. So often, people fear asking for help, or company, or a listening ear, just as much as we fear intruding.

Our "no-strings" offer may open doors we could not imagine. How far we want that door to open is another matter addressed elsewhere in this book. The important thing here is the approach: the decision to make it, the way to make it so that it respects the other person's dignity and presents options, not mandates or curiosity.

This incident also shows how the caring action is shaped by the closeness of the relationship. The woman who rushed up the path was closer to that family and her behavior seemed appropriate. For the rest of us, however, it seemed more appropriate to wait until the door, in a sense, was opened to us by that first neighbor. I remember standing outside and watching the leaves swirl in the chilly wind; watching the blue flicker of television screens through windows. I remember a strong feeling that I could not go back inside my own warm house yet, and I wondered what enabled me to stand there, knowing that sooner or later I would touch my neighbor's grief — against all my East-side, uptown Manhattan upbringing.

I do believe there is an instinct in us all to connect with one another in a caring way, to form community. When we tap into our own well of caring, we image God, who in Christ, told us *we are* one another's neighbors, our brothers' and sisters' keepers.

And, yet, we need certain skills to act on this calling in a way that respects, rather than invades, the other person's boundaries. Offering our very selves, our very presence without demanding an answer, without making

41

our offer conditional is a proven, helpful way. This action, of course, can take more forms than we could name.

The Art of Caring: Coworkers

Some say that we know our coworkers better than our own families. In fact, we often form "work- families" and spend more hours a day with our colleagues than anyone else. On one hand, then, it should be easier to companion a troubled coworker in a caring way, to open the door, to make the approach. On the other hand, unlike purely social relationships, our professional ones are complicated by professional demands, promotions, raises, and job security. What one might confide to a friend may be down-right dangerous to confide to a colleague or supervisor. And so the art of caring in the workplace may be a complex issue.

As I was conceiving this book, someone who works in publishing chuckled darkly: "The art of caring at work. Now wouldn't that be a novel idea," he said, with a touch of bitterness.

Precisely. All the more reason for the art of caring to be practiced there. As with neighbors, we know coworker on different levels. There are friendly acquaintances, there are people who evaluate us and whom we evaluate, close friends with whom we may stay up all night as we work to get a project out on deadline.. There are people we trust, and people we don't.

A friend of mine who is a reporter on a major daily newspaper does not have any close work-friends. Nor does she want any; the atmosphere is too competitive. Were she to need a caring listener, she would turn to a friend or neighbor first. And if someone were to approach her with concern for how she's doing, she admits that she would suspect a hidden agenda.

By contrast, a writer/editor in a high-pressure job situation, which often involved security clearances, felt extremely close to the four other colleagues with whom he worked — so close, in fact, that these men all knew and cared about one another's private circumstances. Tom, the writer / editor I spoke with, was going through a difficult period: divorce, depression, financial worries. Aside from his friendship with his colleagues, he felt utterly isolated.

One of these work-friends offered a concerned, listening ear, and offered much needed emotional, support. With Tom's permission, his work-friend spoke to their superior about the situation in an attempt to get professional help into the picture. The supervisor, they both knew, had gone through clinical depression himself, and would understand — Tom's job would not be jeopardized, especially because Tom's work performance remained high.

However, I believe a note of caution must be sounded here. It can be a tremendous infringement upon another person, his or her reputation and job security if such concerns are voiced without permission. Even with permission, the situation must be carefully weighed. It is often possible to work out solutions, referrals, and other helpful action without involving a supervisor. And, as always, even if no action is taken or agreed upon, you can provide the ministry of presence for your coworker and provide unconditional support. Just knowing that someone cares and is there is powerful.

Sometimes a manager must make a difficult choice regarding a troubled worker. A friend of mine, a managing editor at a small publishing house, was increasingly troubled by sudden absences on the part of a senior editor. As the absences grew more frequent (and always without more than a moment's notice), the senior editor's work began to pile up on my friend's desk. My friend is a bright, highly competent, conscientious person; she is also compassionate. She suspected that her erratic senior editor was a closet alcoholic.

"How should I handle it?" Marilyn asked me one day at lunch. In this case, she felt it would jeopardize her employee to confide her suspicions to anyone else at work. She saw that the editor needed help, but she also knew that she had a schedule to keep, books to get out, and that it was unfair to the other editors to give one preferential treatment. My first suggestion was to talk candidly with her employee, which she did.

The first talk yielded nothing but denial and disclaimer, although for a few weeks the absences diminished. When they resumed, however, Marilyn initi-

44

ated a series of talks and finally the editor admitted that he was indeed struggling with alcoholism.

"It made me sick the night before," Marilyn confided, "but I decided I had to tell him that he could only stay if he went into therapy and to AA. I promised I would go with him to his first appointment. And I did." To her great surprise, the editor stuck with therapy, improved, saved his job, and changed his life.

All stories do not have such stellar endings. It is impossible to force change on someone who is not ready or willing. It is also, I believe, an infringement on that person's boundaries, unless the situation is acutely life-threatening. Marilyn's story, however, remains a striking example to me that the art of caring *can* indeed be practiced along with responsible professionalism.

The editor might have been summarily fired, or might have become a drain on the entire workplace. My friend could have become, in her own words, "a villain or victim," and there were times when she was so out of patience she was tempted by the first role, while other times she wished to avoid confrontation, and was tempted by the second role. In the end, she found a compassionate balance and offered her support and presence to the editor, which turned out to be crucial to his progress.

We have often seen glimmers of this in the workplace: at its best, it is a community where people pull together for someone who is ill, bereaved, or in some other difficulty. In other cases, we have seen productivity and profit come before a more complex, compassionate response. The award-winning movie *Philadelphia* was based on an actual case: a lawyer was fired by his firm when it was discovered that he had AIDS.

In many people's minds, the workplace is a place for hardball, not for caring. It is a place for guardedness, for self-protection, for ignoring the tearful phone call heard through the partition between cubicles. It is a place where many people feel "people with problems have no place." To be sure, it is difficult to live the gospel in the marketplace. It is difficult to take risks when your family depends on your income. "I simply can't afford to be caring — not at work," a friend told me.

I wonder though, in the long run, if we can afford *not* to care. What happens on that barren day when we are out of hope, out of rewards, and, perhaps, just out of a vital relationship? We struggle to keep pace in the marketplace, and there, perhaps more than anywhere, we need to be companioned.

Jesus turned over the money-changers tables at the Temple; he showed anger at those who took advantage of others and showed compassion for the poor who could not afford the price of sacrificial animals. It may be difficult and dangerous for us to take certain stances at work. But, again, it is always possible to simply be present through a caring touch, the talk at lunch, the listening ear. And that, in several cases I know, has made the difference between suicide and life.. The ministry of presence may only be a beginning, but it is something we can always offer, in the workplace, and everywhere else..

More and more people are opting to work at home. Others are willing to sacrifice high salaries and perks for jobs that give their lives a greater sense of meaning. Perhaps they are responding, in part, to the non-caring atmosphere of so many offices, factories, and businesses. Yet I do not think the workplace should ever be considered out of bounds for the art of caring.

This question may require prayerful reflection and exploration in a journal. You may want to draw a diagram of your office and notice "hot spots" (people who may be in difficulty) and "sure spots," (people who are absolutely trustworthy). Then you might want to make a daily, prayerful reflection on where healing is needed in your workplace. You may be able to initiate a dynamic new program, without memos, without promos, without meetings or committees: your own simple practice of the art of caring.

■

<**3**>

The Basics of Caring

Rich is not how much you have ... or where you are
going ... or even what you are.... Rich is who you
have beside you.

— Source unknown

I wanted to curse — I wanted to cry."

The photographer had gone to visit a beloved, retired teacher. "He put my first real camera in my hands," Bill remembered. Somehow, during the past hectic year, they had lost touch. This visit — a surprise — would be a joyful reunion. Bill knocked at the familiar door and waited, juggling his gifts. In the strange silence, he could hear the wind in the trees. And then his mentor's wife opened the door. Squinting into the winter sun, she spoke words that sounded, for an instant, like a foreign language. Her husband had died two months before ... cancer ... went fast....

In his hands, Bill's gifts felt suddenly heavy. "I went numb," he said later. "Then I felt angry, hot. I wanted to curse — I wanted to cry." Instead, he went inside. He sat and "listened, really listened. We both felt better afterwards. But I'll never forget that first minute. It felt like a hundred years."

This story encompasses all the basic elements in the art of caring.

In the midst of busy lives, we try to make our caring show. We try and fail and try again and often find it's not simple, especially with someone close to us. This is what the photographer found as he stood in a doorway and felt his gifts begin to turn to stone in his hands. Somehow, he was able to get through that rough beginning, and past it. "Lucky," he said. "I blow up, sometimes, or freeze." He's not the only one.

In other arts, basic practiced skills are there to undergird the gift. We see this in the painter's sketches, the writer's journal, the dancer's *plies*. And so it is with the art of caring. Here, as well, basic elements of craft help prevent this gift from turning to stone in our hands. These basics can be learned, practiced, and developed in step- by-step patterns. In the art of painting, elements of craft help translate a mental image onto canvas. In the art of caring, specific skills help bring out the caring person within you, with grace under pressure.

The Caring Prism

You can focus your caring, like light through a prism, into strategies that make a difference. There are three elements of craft that are most foundational:

1. A focus on feelings
2. A language of listening
3. A ministry of presence

The art of caring begins with that rugged, messy, glorious terrain which seems least compatible with words like craft and skill: the terrain of your own inner feelings. It is important territory to visit, for grounding and awareness, before you set off toward another country.

1. FOCUS ON FEELINGS

"It is important to feel joy and also to feel pain. And it is critical to feel connected, no matter what gets in the way."
— Peggy Hutchison, *The Sanctuary Movement*

When we think about caring, we usually think of another's feelings first. Perhaps a colleague has lost a job, friends are divorcing, a neighbor is dying, or a spouse struggles with depression. As you read these examples, your focus probably shifts to the person in distress. If you enter each mini-script and play it out, you will discover something else: a kind of emotional "rebound effect." *Your* feelings go into play, like the photographer's when he heard bad news. You may recognize a range of emotions, as he did, or you may be unaware of what swims beneath the surface.

At first, the waters may seem quite calm. You may not want to dive deeper, past clear water and down into the muck. There you might find something slippery, something with teeth: anger, pain, fear, disgust — the urge to run, to cry, to curse. Some old wreck from the past may be down there, or some reaction that makes you feel like a "bad" person.

And so you may stay there, up on the surface, unable to move or connect with another's feelings — because you avoid looking first at your own. Feelings can become roadblocks more easily if we are unaware of them. Bill, the photographer, had to recognize a spectrum of emotions before he could get past them, before he was able to walk through that door.

For many of us, however, this recognition is not a natural, automatic faculty. We may repress or rationalize feelings away; we may react purely from reflex, without thinking, without even knowing what's going on within. Reflexive responses can limit us. That first reaction may reflect panic, self-protection, momentary repulsion. Our first reactions to distress are not always our truest ones.

Replay Bill's story again. How does it look if he yells at the woman, throws the gifts on the porch and stomps away? How does it look if he murmurs chilly regrets and exits, with gifts? Bill, upset that he hadn't been called earlier, realized later that he had considered both of these scenarios. He managed to avoid playing out those scripts "by the seat of my pants," he said. Instead, he took these first basic steps in focusing on feelings.

Stop: Take a Picture

The ability to stop and take stock, even briefly, seems like an art form itself. How often we all say, "If I'd only taken a minute ...." But taking that minute, or five, or whatever, does not have to be some esoteric, exalted ritual. Look at it as a skill, one that can be coaxed forth, cultivated, and practiced until it becomes routine. And it's a useful routine to summon at will. As in external photography, if you want to get a clear picture, you do need to stop and focus — otherwise, all you'll get is a blur.

This kind of blur was experienced recently by a busy professional woman, just after her phone rang at eight in the morning. A friend and neighbor had a problem. He needed to get to a hospitalized parent, but his car would not start. He wondered if he could borrow....

"No," his neighbor found herself saying. She was on her way to work; she had to drive her kids to the sitter.

Her reflex response was a common one: to protect the status quo, to fulfill her daily obligations. Later though, she regretted her choice. Her neighbor's situation wasn't life-or-death emergency, but why did it have to be? As she thought it through, the executive realized she didn't have to be in her office at precisely nine o'clock that one day. She also realized that she might have consulted her husband; he could have driven the neighbor to the hospital. Alternatives, she saw, cannot develop if you don't *stop,* put the phone down or call back, *focus* and *look inward.*

The first question you might ask yourself is: Am I *re*ally threatened by this?

As you react less reflexively and more intentionally to distress, you may find that structured routines have grown very powerful in your life. They hold things together, provide a sure path and perhaps, a kind of bulwark against chaos, internal and external. Sometimes, if they grow inflexible, they may also become roadblocks to the art of caring.

Others find their road blocks are sheer emotion. A business man feels paralyzed before a hospital visit to a dying relative; he can make deals and negotiate with clients, but the thought of that hospital room makes him give a reflex, "no-time" answer. Later, when he looks within, he sees fear of his own mortality

"When I stopped and took that 'inside picture,'" a friend reports, "I didn't see fear. What I saw was revulsion. Me? I didn't realize how repelled I am by *messiness* in people, messy out-of-control behavior. It makes me cringe, as if I'll get swept out of control, too. So I stepped back from this friend's divorce. Now it's too late."

Perhaps not; not in terms of that situation, and certainly not for others, waiting up ahead. I believe that we can train ourselves to stop, take time, and look inside. But how exactly do we take that look?

Emptying

This technique is sometimes used in therapy. It also happens to be a technique I use when I teach fiction-writing, though I've never named it. Many writers and journal-keepers are familiar with the practice of emptying feelings out onto paper. These are private notes, kept daily: a page or two, for your eyes only, recorded before your day begins in earnest. What does one write on these pages? Whatever is on your mind, spilled freely, without stopping, without self-editing. Often, this acts as a kind of clearing device, surfacing anxieties, resentments, as well as ideas, hopes, and dreams. Write intentionally without a censor, so you can express your feelings honestly, without fear.

As you practice the art of caring, you will, of course, run into the feelings of others. It is especially important, then, to be clear about your own, in whatever situation you face. Unclaimed feelings can block you, ambush you, or get projected onto others. Emptying may provide a safe way to externalize emotions, to take an inner snapshot and see what's there.

Suspending Judgment

You have a right to your feelings. As children, we are taught to classify them as "good" and "bad," but we can relearn this pattern and avoid the labels. The practice here is one of detachment. You are taking inventory. You are viewing your own inner snapshot, at this time. With detachment, you can do this more accurately, not as an armchair psychoanalyst, but as preparation for action.

Look closely; identify roadblocks and "hooks, " as my crisis hotline trainer used to call them. Sooner or later, she told us, we would all get "hook" calls — the ones that would reel us in by hooking into a painful memory, a vulnerability, or some issue that always makes us mad. There would be other situations which would draw out our strengths; it was important to know them, too, and tap into them. We were asked to make a private inventory of those areas so we could be prepared. For me, this deliberate form of preparation, this intentional survey of firm and marshy inner ground, is one of the most helpful tools I was given on the way to helping others.

On your way, as you practice, you will run more easily, more quickly, through these first basic steps: *stop, focus, "empty"* (take inventory), and *identify* blocks, hooks and strengths. Then wrap up this part of the process with one more technique; one that takes up all the strands and ties them together.

Put Them Over There

You have made yourself aware of your inner landscape; what do you do with that now, as you move on toward someone else's terrain?

I remember a gifted mentor (the head chaplain at the D.C. jail) telling us to prepare for each day as chaplains by clearing our inner selves. This did not mean erasing who we were. It did not mean becoming blank, indifferent human cut-outs. It meant, he said, "putting it all over there" — the knee-jerk reflexes, all the doubts and blocks we had worked so hard to identify.

To illustrate, he asked us to imagine taking off a coat and hanging it on a hook by the door: "Put it over there, with all its pockets, linings, stuff." This chaplain, seasoned and graced, also had a dry sense of humor. "No one wants your coat," he said. "It'll be there when the day's over. Meanwhile, hang it up, put it over there. That's what you do with some of your own stuff — *if it gets in the way.*"

How exactly do you "put it over there"? The image itself has helped me and others. It may also be helpful to visualize your "stuff" as a package, placed on a safe shelf. The conscious decision to summon this image, in full detail, can be powerful; deliberate choices put us in control. It's also reassuring to know where "your stuff" is. It's wise to be attentive to it.

And it's tremendously liberating to put it over there, for now, if it gets in the way of helpful caring. You may "put it over there" more than once in certain situations; that's to be expected. This is not a single gesture, but a practice — a practice that frees up more of your energy and spirit for the next basic element in the art of caring.

One thing that can help us to "put it over there" is to remember that ill or troubled people behave in ways that sometimes may appear negative, perhaps even hostile. My supervisor in my training as a chaplain emphasized, that we need to resist the temptation to take such behavior personally; the person in difficulty may be experiencing, tremendous frustration, fear, and a loss of control. These emotions may come out as anger, displaced onto the nearest person, but this anger, frustration, or fear is really directed at the person's situation.

For example, I recall a hospital patient who threw his bedpan from his, room into the hallway. I was chaplain on that floor and when I reported this incident to my supervisor, he smiled kindly and said to me, "I hope you know that bedpan was hurled at sickness itself, not at you."

2. A LANGUAGE OF LISTENING

"Do you hear? That is the grass harp,
always telling a story — it knows the stories
of all the people ... who have ever lived, and
when we are dead it will tell ours, too."
    — Truman Capote, *The Grass Harp,*

"What do I do?" asked the new hospital chaplain.

"You listen," his supervisor told him.

"But what do I *do?"*

"You listen."

For many of us, listening seems passive — a kind of non-action. Gifted interviewers, clergy, teachers, counselors, and lawyers think of listening quite differently, however. And as you begin to listen actively, intentionally, you may never hear things the same way again. You start to hear what Truman Capote's characters heard in *The Grass Harp:* fragments of the human story. Each time you practice the art of caring, you will hear another fragment, another phrase, and this will become a gift to you, a whole series of gifts.

Listening is also the gift you give to someone in difficulty or distress., in the midst of a crisis or a problem. Unfortunately, it seems to be a half-forgotten gift. Sometime, someplace, every one of us has heard these words:

"All I wanted was someone to listen...."

If the language of listening has grown foreign to many, I believe we can re-learn it. As humans, we have a good ear for it, still.

Active Listening

The concept of active listening may sound at first like a contradiction in terms. In fact, I believe it is listening in its best, most authentic state. Think about this as you list the qualities you associate with good listening.

Many of us would list *attentiveness, along with eye-contact,,* and *interest* as important qualities. You may express interest simply by your expression, or by those small, responsive sounds people offer as part of the dialogue: not bored grunts, but brief empathetic punctuation. For some people, an "Ahhh" speaks a whole sentence of concern.. For others, a nod, or a simple "yes" to underscore a point, conveys a paragraph's worth of words.

I never quite realized how important active listening is in everyday life until I worked on a hotline. Voices came through the phone, out of the night, and I had to respond as I listened, if only to let the callers know I was still with them. Afterwards, as a hospital chaplain, in dim rooms late at night, the same sort of dialogue evolved.

If someone could not see my face, it was especially important to respond in small ways: small enough so as not to interrupt; tangible enough to say, without words, "I'm here, I'm with you." Listen as if the other person cannot see your face, and respond with sound. At the same time, listen as if you were mute, and respond with your eyes, your face, your gestures.

Total silence may seem daunting, disapproving. Partial silence, however, can be grace-filled. If you let the silence be part of the language's rhythms, it will open space for reflection, and time for the speaker to hear her own words echo, sometimes bringing insight with them. For me, this has been a great privilege to witness, every time it happens, and no time is the same.

Active listening means concentration. It means empathy, expressed through eyes and face and those small sounds we humans make. Through the dark night of the soul, it is a way to speak without speaking. It is a way of saying without words, "I'm with you.... Someone knows, someone hears; someone cares."

Reflective Listening

Imagine a mirror that acts as a window. Reflective listening can be just that. It began as a counseling technique and it is another helpful tool for practicing the art of caring. Like all tools, it needs to be used wisely, respectfully, and with compassion. It can be illuminating or mocking; that depends on the one who uses the tool. Reflective listening, as its name implies, reflects back to the speaker emotional content in the speech.

As we talk, we may hear our own lyrics but miss the music underneath them. We may hear the facts we relate, but not their subtexts. A skilled listener can hear both and help the speaker note them, too. Reflective listening opens up deeper areas with nonjudgmental statements or restatements of what the listener hears on other levels. This technique is particularly helpful for people swamped in confusing feelings.

"Sounds really frustrating," you might say to a person who is angry, helpless — frustrated indeed, but not entirely aware of it. And he may say, "Damn frustrating, let me tell you...." Your words give him some needed permission to let it all out, at last.

"What a dilemma — do you feel caught?" You might reflect back to someone else, with empathy that may release the speaker's pent-up tears.

Reflective listening is a way to empathize, to show your solidarity with someone else. It is also a language that shows respect: it does not preach or judge or dish out uninvited advice. Like all languages, this one takes practice, and as you use it, you will find how well it can empower others, helping them to hear not only their own words but their music as well. New insights often arise.

Listening on the Feeling Level

In our left-brained, high-tech, fast-lane culture, we tend to listen with our heads more than our spirits. "Listen with the eyes of the heart," the Bible tells us, and there is a longing for this, especially when people talk about their feelings. You saw before, as you focused on your own feelings, how vulnerable you can feel in that process. That foundational exercise helps you understand why it is crucial to avoid trivializing or judging someone else's feelings. These emotions often need to be heard and honored before anything else can happen. It is also important to be aware that the process of listening can, eventually, bog down here, in the feelings. The listener will begin to hear a circular pattern. Only if the earlier, inner work has been done thoroughly will the listener recognize such circularity as a common human pattern.

Helpful listeners, I believe, hold opposites in balance: they use complementary faculties at once, listening with head *and* heart, empathy *and* detachment It is not cold detachment, not patronizing tolerance, but the detachmended of real caring: standing close, standing back, standing close yet again, in an endless dance that brings caring into play.

At first, you may feel you can't hold both opposites in tension at once. Notice, though, how you are reading this page, having that question, and hearing sounds down the hail or outside — all at one time. You know that you can hold many disparate elements in balance as you think while driving, cooking, shaving. Listening on levels is a more advanced form, but one based in what you already know. The more you practice, the more levels you will hear. You can begin with your very next conversation.

Consider keeping a "listener's log." I was required to do this as I trained for chaplaincy and the log was enormously useful; over a period of time, it showed me certain patterns I could not discern at the time. During this training I was also required to write up a "verbatim" after certain visits to patients. In a verbatim (from the Latin, "word for word"), you record, without explanation or comment, what was said in a given interchange. It should be written as soon as possible after the conversation. It comes out looking like a piece of dialogue unfit for Hollywood (most of the time).

Don't worry about sounding brilliant; your concern is what you heard and how helpful your responses were. Did you give the other person room to talk? Did you create a receptive atmosphere? Did you take over, or grow distant? What did you hear, as words: as music? Gradually, your will discover sudden moments of breakthrough, connection, and insight: the greatest gifts a listener can give..

Again, the tools are in your hands; the skills, are here to practice: active listening, reflective listening, listening "with the eyes of the heart," a listener's log, and the verbatim. When listening; becomes: a language, it becomes the art of caring.

3. THE MINISTRY OF PRESENCE

"... You sit with your friend, and all at once a silence falls on speech, and his eyes; without a flicker, glow at you. You two have seen the Secret together, and there you sit, ... catching a little whiff of the ether reserved for God himself"
— Edgar Lee Masters

Faith Matheny's Epitaph, *Spoon River Anthology*

If there is one essential element in the art of caring, it is the ministry of presence., My *supervisor taught this.* concept to a small group of us, training for chaplaincy in a city hospital. The concept sounded somewhat: vague:; mere sentiment, not the, "do-something" approach we wanted then. We didn't understand, at first, the sheer power of presence. Later, I was amazed by its quiet steadfast force and versatility. I remain awed as I see this principle illuminate situations far beyond hospitals, be yond all boundary lines: wherever there are human beings living their lives amidst others.

As, we practice the art of caring, we face a wide range situations, personalities, and dynamics. The ministry of presence, however, is one of those rarities that spans. then, all, as a basic stance, a way of being with a person in distress. I say that not only from my own experience but from the experience of seasoned practitioners of the caring arts. In our "Can-Do Fix-It" Western culture, the ministry of presence may seem, at first, deceptively simple.

Being There

The emphasis is on *being* fully present with another, more than *doing* something directly for another. Of course, the doing is contained in your focused presence — in your being there. When you companion another in distress, confusion, pain, loss, you undertake a journey of the spirit. You walk with someone who is burdened.

You are not there to lift the burden off, but rather to walk the path together, to support that person *and* that burden with your steady presence. If it's possible to lift, it will be best for your companion to do it himself, when he is stronger, when he is ready.

Sound easy? Try it. To be fully present is to stay fully focused on another — and we may discover, to our chagrin, that our attention spans are shorter than we'd thought. It may require tremendous self-control to be there with someone, simply be there, without doing something immediately.

I recall a chaplain-intern, upset after a visit to a patient. "If I can't fix it, why be there?" the intern blurted out. His supervisor looked unsurprised: "Can you fix the patient's cancer?"

There was a silence. "Then what *can* I do?" Like a wise abbot, the supervisor held his trainee's gaze. "You can be there. You can be there, with him, in the dark."

Recently, a woman spoke to me with concern for her daughter who was out of college and on her own, "having a rough time." The woman wanted desperately to help, to lift burdens, to make things better — a natural maternal response. Except that it wasn't helping; in fact, it seemed to be making things worse. Visits turned into a pattern: mother gives advice, daughter gets mad, mother get mad, visit ends with upset and estrangement ... until the cycle would repeat again.

Then, after learning about the ministry of presence, the worried mother brought it into her next visit. This took self-discipline, she said, "But I never would have believed how comforting it was for both of us. Just being together. I listened and for maybe half an hour, we just sat in silence — good silence. I think she felt my love coming through in a different way. Her defensive walls are starting to come down. I feel hopeful again...."

The ministry of presence seems to open communication lines. Why? It does not put the other person on the defensive, as this story shows. The practice also shows respect for this person, as she is, whatever the circumstances are. Finally, this presence is a patient discipline. There are times when others are simply not able to move on to solutions. No matter what we say, they won't hear us. Until they can, we can be there with them; we can be there for them. And sometimes, in that atmosphere, many forms of healing can begin.

Calling Forth Stories

As a teacher of writing, I have come to believe story-telling is part of the human condition. Which of us has never told a story? We tell them often, sometimes without knowing what we're doing — or without knowing that our stories tell themselves back to us again; if we listen, we may hear comfort, or caution, or wisdom. You give a gift when you call forth someone's story; you provide the witness in a time of trouble, to reclaim a time of strength, or joy, or inspiration. Such stories are deep wells, present within each of us, there to draw on for life-giving water. They are also part of the practice of "being there," part of the ministry of presence.

Following Up

Steadfast, caring presence creates trust. You know this from your own experience, and so do I. Continuity helps build trust and with that trust, an atmosphere in which growth and change can happen. If we reject someone for being in difficulty, in distress, in troubled times, I believe we do something very damaging — to that person and, ultimately, to ourselves.

Sometimes, maintaining the ministry of presence takes a great deal of strength. We get frustrated, we grow weary, we feel angry that the person won't move at our pace. When this happens, it is important to go back to your earlier work with "the basics" of caring. Get clear on your feelings; "empty" your feelings into writing or a tape recorder. Talk to someone outside the situation, as we talked to our supervisors on the hotline and in the hospital. Take care of yourself, and your own feelings, so that you can go on practicing the ministry of presence.

That non-abandoning presence is one of the factors that makes a difference. It is possible even in certain cases in which professional intervention is necessary. And that kind of presence is, in turn, made possible by other, undergirding basics.

68

Widening the Support System

If it isn't already in place, or in sight, involve other people in a supportive network. Working together, everyone can keep turning the wheel of caring. If the situation is long-term, you will not be able to turn that wheel alone. Respect for confidentiality is essential, but it helps you, as well as your fellow traveler, to have a wide network in action: friends, family, community, and if appropriate, professional help as well. As you involve others, you want be clear on this point: you are not abandoning this person you walk with; you are widening the caring circle. He or she may need to be reassured of that.

Let Visiting Take Many Forms

If you can't be with a person "in the flesh," there are many other ways to practice a ministry of presence. One of my mentors, an older woman, deeply seasoned in the art of caring, thought of flowers as "the ambassadors of the soul." Whenever she received them, she placed them in whatever room she occupied so they could "keep her company."

She was very good at writing small, frequent notes from wherever she was — a museum, a theater, a train, the office, a park, or a church; notes that said, "I'm thinking of you in my daily life, no matter how busy I am," purely by their frequency and range. In addition, she tried to send notes that brought her surroundings to the recipient: a museum note card, a theater program, a postcard photo of a church where she had lit a candle for the person in her thoughts.

Things you make are wonderful conveyors of presence, whether you bake or sew or draw or do crafts. And if you do none of these things, or none of them well, your efforts will be genuine and fresh and original.

Things that widen the world may also bring your presence to the person on your mind: books or books of pictures, photographs, clippings which you know will be of interest — and won't preach. Again, this is a way to maintain steady connection, just as much as the regular phone call. I think "regular" is a guiding word here. It matters more than how pretty the note card, how lavish the flowers, how absolutely right a gift may be for its recipient.

Thoughtfulness cannot be undervalued in gift-giving; but what mediates your steadfast caring, on a regular basis, creates and maintains a ministry of presence when you can't be there in person.

A ministry of presence, then, begins with an emphasis on *being with* rather than *doing for; companioning* rather than fixing. It means a *steadfast, nonjudgmental stance,* with the understanding that trust and healing grow in that atmosphere. And only in that atmosphere can you eventually ask harder questions (see Chapter 4, "The Language of Caring").

A ministry of presence is not a quick fix; nor is it problem-solving, which comes later. And because this practice *isn't* quick, we need to set our expectations accordingly. Ultimately, a ministry of presence respects the other person's dignity and autonomy. This respect for the person communicates belief in the person, which may be sustaining, until the person can again believe in herself or himself again. As you "practice the presence," you will find yourself building on earlier skills: a focus on feelings and a language of listening. You may also find creative ways to maintain your presence with someone when you cannot be there in person.

Whether you are religious or not, spiritually inclined or not, there is a custom which seems appropriate here. The Society of Friends, known more widely as Quakers, have a practice called "holding someone in the Light." For the Friends, this is a kind of visual prayer, in which someone is held in God's love and illuminating presence. For you, this may be helpful as a practice or simply as a concept.

When we hold someone in our thoughts with care, a great *deal* follows naturally from *there,* in terms of our actions. And whenever we hold someone in "the Light," as we see it, we are giving yet another form to our ministry of presence — and to the art of caring.

The basics of caring begin a process, always growing, sometimes in surprising ways. You may find yourself stretching; you may find yourself doing what you thought was impossible. You may also find yourself returning to the basic elements of your craft, again and again, as the dancer returns to the barre, the painter to the sketch pad.

On those days when muscles are sore and sketches seem botched, you may want to quit. Most artists do.

I have found, though, that — if you keep practicing, at some surprising juncture you will come upon moments shot through with wonder, moments that stun you, lift you, and make the world oddly new.

I remember a late afternoon in January, when winter darkness deepened around a woman in a purple coat. Unemployed, elderly, middle-class, she had not been able to keep up with her rent and hadn't wanted to ask for help. I remember how she glanced back at the ground floor apartment, from which she had just been evicted. The city's truck had taken her furniture off the street. Remaining was one end of a dining table, the kind with leaves, a chipped lamp, and an easy chair where its owner sat as I approached.

Summoned by my church, I had come with hastily heated food: canned soup in a thermos and a frozen apple turnover I had almost burned. I had also come with my own plan — I thought I knew exactly what this woman needed: dinner in the warm parish hall, then transport to the only shelter in the city with an available bed on this cold night.

Jenny, I'll call her. She looked up at me from that chair where she had sat, no doubt, to read, to watch TV. She could not bring herself to leave it now, she told me. Not yet. Not just yet. She gripped the chair's soft arms and in the cold, her face shown with perspiration. Her skin was the color of pale tallow, her eyes startling blue.

She'd been a writer once, she said. I smiled — grimly. Jenny's blue gaze scanned the remnants of a household: a Mexican-style candle stick, a potted plant, three red cloth napkins.

I wondered what I was doing here at all, with bag of bad food and my notions of what was best for this woman I barely knew. But Jenny knew what was best for her right now: staying with her things, just a little while — "so I can leave them," she said, gazing at her magazines, splayed on the cement. "Can't explain it." She ran a hand over her damp face.

And so we sat at that table's end, where she spread out a red, cloth napkin and I lit the candle and, over the heated convenience food, sitting on the street, Jenny said grace. In the January dusk, commuters passed, staring, as we had dinner for two, Jenny and I, on the sidewalk. She ate heartily and fast and her hand trembled as she lifted her fork into the chilly air. I did nothing; Jenny did it all.

She spoke of other bad times and remembered, abruptly, how she'd gotten through them. She spoke of her mother's courage and her father's death and of a summer when, as a young woman, for a boat ride on the river, she had worn a wide-brimmed hat, "the color of fresh snow." Church bells rang eight o'clock. The shelter would hold that bed for one more hour. I could not force them to wait, nor could I force Jenny to move. I'd seen people choose the streets over a shelter — out of pride, fear, obstinacy. By eight-thirty, the candle sputtered, burning down. The church rang the half-hour.

"Jenny," I began, then stopped. Chin high, she was rising from the table. Like a queen, she cloaked herself in her own dignity. Once more, she scanned the chair — all the remains. "Looks like a shipwreck." She blew out the candle. "I'm not going down with it." We drove to the shelter. Overhead, as Jenny walked forward, the bells of a different church rang nine o'clock.

Practicing the Basics

Focus on Feelings

1. Try the practice of "emptying" on a regular basis, every morning, for one week to see if this is helpful for you. Write one or two pages of whatever is on your mind, as close to awakening as possible. Once you've had this practice, you will find it easier to use the technique in specific situations. It may be helpful to keep a special notebook for this — and for your eyes only.

2. After you gone through the steps suggested in the chapter's first segment — stop, focus, take inventory — draw a sketch of your "inner snapshot" of emotions at the time. Then draw another. Do you see a change in the two sketches? Does one seem less anxiety-producing? Note your feelings.

3. Practice the visualization of "putting it over there." Notice especially what "it" is for you — a coat, a package, a hat, a ball of wool, etc. If this is difficult to visualize, write a brief scene in which you enter a room where someone waits for you, someone in need of caring. Near the door are coat-hooks and a rack where items may be kept. As you narrate the scene in writing, the images may come more easily. If there is resistance, note that, but try the scene in the third person, from someone else's point of view.

4. Make a list of all the strengths you bring to the art of caring. It is very important to focus on what you do well, even as you become aware of possible roadblocks. Practice playing from your strengths, after you have put the blocks "over there."

A Language of Listening

1. Write a verbatim of any conversation you have had in the last twenty-four hours. Write in the form of dialogue, starting each speaker's new sentence with his or her initials, and head what you say with your own. Leave in all the "urns," "uh-huhs," and silences. This will help you "hear" yourself in conversation with another.

2. Look over your verbatim and mark it up as a special kind of editor would: note where you listened well, where you may have tuned out, interrupted, or switched the

focus before the other person was ready. Highlight the strong areas.

3. Next, note the areas in which you practiced active listening responses. These may come in those "uh-huhs" and small words we may omit as we record the exchange.

4. Note also places where you have used reflective listening. This is a skill that needs practice, so you might intentionally use it in upcoming conversations — the grist for another verbatim, or several, and the kind of analysis outlined here. I might add that these are the same exercises we were given as chaplains-in-training in a big city hospital, in a specialized program administered by seasoned professionals.

The Ministry of Presence

1. Practice being with someone in this way, especially someone to whom you may tend to dispense unsolicited advice, judgment, etc. If this is difficult, try it for a half-hour and then an hour, as did the worried mother cited in this chapter. She began with a half-hour and expanded the time from there. "Just being there" does not have to mean silence, though it may include silence.

2. Make notes to yourself after this time is over. What did you notice? Were you comfortable? Did you feel awkward? Was there a quiet deepening of a bond, the

creation of one — or perhaps nothing visible happened at all. Don't expect a "big experience" immediately Every situation and relationship, of course, has its own timing.

3. If you were to design a logo or symbol for the ministry of presence, what would it look like to you? Open hands? Clasped hands? Other images entirely? Sketch — without judging.

4. Write a paragraph or a page about a time in your life when someone was simply "there for you." Try to recapture the details, to visualize it again, and articulate why and how it was helpful. Now, reverse the roles in this memory and imagine yourself as the one "being there" for this person who was present this way with you.

5. Reward yourself for coming this far. As you go on in the practice of the art of caring, you may find the reward is in the experience itself, in special moments of connection and communion. There will also be times, especially at the start, where there is nothing tangible happening at all. Even so, you have chosen a special course and dared to undertake a special journey.

Do something for yourself that signifies your recognition of that fact. Buy yourself a flower to remind you of this as you sit at your desk. Buy a good notebook for your sketches and logs. Do something that lifts your spirits, whatever that is for you, and as you experience the lift, know that in many different ways, you will be helping to "midwife" this feeling in others.

■

<4>

The Language of Caring

If I speak in the tongues of angels, but do not have
love, I am a noisy gong or a clanging cymbal.
— 1 Corinthians 13:1

Ididn't say anything because I didn't know what to say."
How often have we said those words to ourselves? A
friend, coworker, or neighbor is in difficulty, and as much
as we may want to speak words of consolation or offer
help or sympathy, words fail us. And quite often, in the
end, we say nothing. Sometimes this leaves us with
life-long regret, coupled with frustration.

A striking example of this occurred a couple of years ago to a businesswoman I know, a lovely, compassionate, capable person. A colleague of hers, in the same field but in a different company, ran into her regularly at various professional gatherings. Mary Ann knew that this man, recently divorced, had an emotionally troubled sister who had made an attempt at suicide. Since then, the sister's progress had been up and down. Mary Ann's colleague often invited her "to meet for lunch sometime." She, however, always found some reason to say no. She told herself that it was inappropriate for her, a married woman, to have lunch with a single, male colleague.

In retrospect, however, she realized that "doing lunch" is such a commonplace in business that her excuse shamed her. After a few months of refusals, Mary Ann heard that her colleague's sister had indeed committed suicide. The businesswoman was stricken; she realized that her male colleague had probably wanted to talk to her about the worsening situation and that she had not known what to say and so avoided the whole challenge.

She tried to rationalize her choice by telling herself that in any event there was nothing she could have done to prevent the situation. Yet it gnawed at her enough that she discussed it with me. As she talked it through, she realized that she, a woman whose business was words, had not known what to say, had felt inadequate, and so said nothing. Further, she realized, that she could have helped her colleague by simply listening to him and making him feel less alone; perhaps her presence might have given him the strength to try other options. There were no implications that he had wanted anything else from her, and now she felt haunted by what she had left unsaid.

How often we all feel haunted by the echo of unspoken words. And how easy it is for us to rationalize that what little we might say couldn't make any real difference. The businesswoman found, in the wake of this tragedy, that her presence was of great solace to the bereaved male colleague. She indeed offered a "ministry of presence," discussed in the last chapter — simply the act of listening.

Discernment

Like this businesswoman, we all face moments when we must decide if and how to become involved with a person in need. How do we make prudent judgments on whether or not to intervene? These judgments often put us into a delicate balance, where common sense may not be quite enough.

One kind of decision process is intuitive: listen to your gut reaction. However, it is important to balance this with some cerebral input. For example, your gut reaction may be, "Oh, no! this will mess up my day. I'm afraid I can't handle this," while your head may say, "Calm down, you can do it. There is a solution."

The famous Myers-Briggs Personality-Type test posits that some people react more intuitively than others who react more on the basis of factual information. The test, however, points out that we all have recessive strengths or abilities in the non-dominant areas of our personalities. To illustrate, I am intuitive, yet I often use logic to "reality test" or balance a "feeling" I have about something. My hope for you is that you would be able to integrate responses from your head and heart as you weigh the factors in a decision to intervene.

I would add, however, the words of a wise priest and mentor, after he spoke at length with a homeless person who approached him. As we walked away, the priest smiled at me. "Sometimes it's hard to know what to do," he said. "I guess I always prefer to err on the side of compassion."

On a retreat, I learned a visual prayer, which has often helped me with the matter of discernment about what to do. Perhaps it will be helpful to you. The retreat director invited us to close our eyes and visualize Jesus or Mary, or perhaps a saint or angel standing before us. Sometimes the image will come on its own; sometimes you will select it. The retreat director encouraged us to draw near to the figure with whom we feel the greatest freedom in being ourselves.

Some people, for example, felt very close to Jesus and saw him as a healer. Others felt a bit daunted by an intimate visualization involving Jesus and felt more open and free with an image of a saint, or a guardian angel. Still others felt more comfortable with a female, maternal image, and so chose the Virgin Mary. Next the retreat director encouraged us to see the troubled person and/or the problem materialize before us.

Quite often, the director counseled, the problem may take visual form. In my visualization, it manifested itself as a tangled skein of yarn — so tangled and knotted I could not begin to unravel it. Someone else visualized a problem as a clod of dried, crusted earth. We were to visualize ourselves as taking the person or the problem, in its symbolic form, in our hands.

Sometimes, I should note, the troubled person also took on a symbolic appearance: a lamb, a wilting flower, a flickering candle. We were asked to pray that God would guide us, and then we were asked to hand over what we held to the divine figure before us. I gave my skein of yarn to Jesus; the person with the clod of earth gave it over to a shining archangel.

Then the retreat director told us to stay and watch; often at this point, as the problem or person changed hands, the symbol itself might begin to change. If it did not, we were told not to be concerned or to think we had failed. Rather, we were urged to see this as the first step in a prayerful, caring process, and to "look in" on the problem in the hands of the Holy One from time to time throughout the coming days.

This exercise in visual prayer is more effective with some people than others, although many people who termed themselves nonvisual or not imaginative, were often quite surprised at their ability to pray in this way.

And some of them experienced a growth that they hadn't expected.

For example, the man who had handed over the clod of earth saw this dry, crusty ball begin to soften and sprout green shoots. I saw the skein of yarn transform itself into a beautiful, glistening spider web, arranged in orderly lines, lit by dew and sunlight. For other people, however, traditional prayer, praying the psalms, or contemplative, discursive, or verbal prayer were of great help in the process of discernment.

The Art of Listening

"Is anyone there? Is anyone listening?"

I wasn't listening to Peggy. Often, I would take a walk through the neighborhood. Sitting there, a lone figure with a red ribbon in her wispy gray hair, was an old woman gazing hopefully at the hummingbird feeder on her porch. Later, she told me that the color red attracts hummingbirds and so she wore a red hair-ribbon as she waited for the winged creatures she especially loved.

It took me longer than it should have to realize that Peggy was waiting also for some human creature to stop and simply listen to her for a few minutes. When I finally walked up her path to talk with her, I learned a great deal: about crippling rheumatoid arthritis, about her time in the WAVES during World War II ... and about hummingbirds. I also learned, first hand, the power of a listening presence; just fifteen minutes and Peggy's face was alight. She had affirmed aloud who she was, remembered her proud past, and, above all, connected with another human being.

I did very little; I simply stood there and listened. When the day came that I passed her house and the porch was empty, I was so very grateful that I had — and horrified at the all the other opportunities I had missed, rationalizing my brisk stride and brisker wave with the schedule "I had to keep," the number of pages "I had to write," the number of phone calls "I had to return." Sometimes, after I had begun to stop at Peggy's porch, we would simply be together in companionable silence.

Now, I remember the silences as well as the talk and the red ribbon. Every time I see a bird feeder, I think of Peggy and I give thanks. Before I received any training in pastoral care, there was Peggy: my first teacher in the art of caring communication.

Someone to Listen

"Is anyone listening? Is anybody there?"

We say this quite often in the course of our everyday lives, but, perhaps, until we have a serious difficulty and try to recount it to someone reading a newspaper, to someone whose eyes stray to his watch, to someone who can be heard turning magazine pages on the other end of the phone line — we do not realize the incredible power of focused, active listening. Many people I have counseled and many friends have said, in a voice rising close to a wail, *"I just want someone to listen."* And so do we all. Listening: it seems elementary. It was not until I was trained to work on a large, metro hotline that I realized how complex an art good listening is. I would like to share some of this training with you.

First, listening does not mean simply attentive silence. It means eye contact, those small noises we make to say, in essence, "I'm with you; I'm hearing you." It means focused attention which does not make the speaker feel you are really planning dinner or watching the clock or rushing the conversation along. And it does involve facial expressions and body language, which are open, sympathetic, and attentive. Crossed arms over the chest, fidgeting hands, glances at clocks, frequent interruptions, especially to argue or finish sentences, can convey an attitude of distraction, disinterest, or even irritation.

If you practice the art of listening as a kind of meditation, you will find it requires effort. Although we sometimes imagine it as passive or nonresponsive, the art of caring translated into listening is, as we saw in Chapter Three, indeed active and powerful. Sometimes, when I listen to a person's story, I want to take out my editor's blue pencil and eliminate the digressions, the seemingly irrelevant asides, and what may appear to be tangents.

Later, however, I have come to realize that those tangents, asides, and digressions contain valuable pieces of the story. In many cases they are, in fact, central, not marginal notes. In any case, people need to tell their stories in their own style, at their own pace — not ours. As a writer, as well as a pastoral caregiver, I recognize the incredible richness of a story told as the storyteller sees it. I would not cut details for fear of eviscerating the tale's power.

The practice of listening is exactly that: a practice. And as we grow more skilled at it, we become the privileged witness to wondrous, sometimes humorous windows into the human condition. Another important dimension to the art of listening is to listening for feelings. These may be veiled in anecdote or explanation. Emily Dickinson said of another writer, "She has the facts, but not the phosphorescence." The facts, of course, do not tell the whole story; you cannot know a person from his or her resume.

Reflective Listening

As you practice the art of listening, you may want to try what we called in the last chapter "reflective listening." This is a nondirective, nonjudgmental tech-nique pioneered by Carl Rogers. In reflective listening, as the name suggests, you reflect back what you hear. This does not mean you become an echo, but that you pick up on certain feeling-words and help the speaker to recognize them. This may be done in a clinical way, for example, "You sound pretty angry. What I hear you saying is you're frightened." Or it can be done in a way that seems to me a bit less distanced, a bit more human and colloquial, "Gosh, how frustrating for you," or, "Gee, that must be hard." Sometimes the listener will tell you if you are reflecting back the wrong emotion; sometimes the speaker will nod, his eyes filling, and say "Yes, exactly. You know what I mean."

In my experience in chaplaincy, these clicks of recognition have been so powerful, they seem to carry an electrical charge. Suddenly, a glaze seems to vanish from the other person's eyes, which fill not only with tears but with light. The person feels *understood* — *and* so, no longer alone.

Open-Ended Questions

As you build on the practice of active and reflective listening, you will also want to build other skills. On the hotline, in chaplaincy at a hospital and a prison, in nursing homes and homeless shelters alike, I was taught that it is far more important to empower the other person than to step in and give advice, pass judgment, or impose my own solutions. This is equally true when we are dealing with neighbors, friends, and coworkers. In these cases, however, it is often more difficult to resist the temptation to be directive. It's easier and quicker to handle many situations that way. But in the end, I truly believe that it is not to the other person's advantage.

Quite often the answers lie within that person, but in times of trouble those answers are hard to see. It is tremendously liberating to reach down inside oneself and find that the well is not dry. The emotional bank balance is not overdrawn, "I am not the basket-case I thought." It is a miracle to watch people regain their own power, self-esteem, and ability to heal. This can happen if we, the listener, the companion in the art of caring can offer ourselves up as catalysts and "midwives" in the process.

There are certain phrases, a kind of psychosocial jargon that may facilitate this process:

• How are you doing with that?

• Are you in a good place with that?

• How do you feel about that?

• When I hear you say that, I hear....

Sometimes these phrases are very effective in eliciting emotion and giving the speaker a chance to shape his or her own thoughts. Sometimes, however, there is an artificiality about some of these phrases in certain situations. Perhaps I feel this because I've been so trained in their usage. As a hospital chaplain, when I visited terminally ill cancer patients who told me about their illnesses, I found it pretty hard to say, "So you're dying of cancer, how do you feel about that?" It is important, even as we struggle for the right way to say something, not to demean the other person accidentally.

One way to be helpful is to ask open-ended questions — in proportion to the situation. You want to meet the person on the "feeling level," the level of the emotions. A caring response before the question, such as, "Gosh, you're really facing something tough. How's it going?" may be more helpful than the more clinical, "How do you feel about that?"

Whatever you say, your words have the greatest healing power when they come from the heart and address the person's emotions, not his or her philosophy, analytic abilities, or tasks to be faced. In times of stress, conflict, or adversity, acute or otherwise, we tend to respond first with our emotions — however we may stonewall, however we may tell ourselves that grownups don't "lose it." First and foremost, therefore, people's emotions must be tended and respected. And in our culture, it is precisely those emotions that we would often rather avoid. One of the best ways to touch those emotions, and touch them gently, respectfully, is to frame an open-ended question.

You may want to compose a list of these and keep adding to it. Here are some examples which I have found extremely helpful in various cases:

• "I'm wondering if ...?"

• "Do you think you might be ...?"

- "It's my sense, just listening to you, that perhaps ...?"

- "Could it be that you're feeling ...?"

- "How's it going?"

- "How are you doing?"

On the other hand, in this practice of the art of caring communication, it is advisable to avoid judging or advice-giving. All my supervisors have cautioned against certain statements which tend to preach, judge, or trivialize another person's difficulty. When I was a chaplain, my supervisor showed me a list of such statements, quite often pronounced by clergy, caregivers, or family friends — statements which, in the face of death, suffering, depression, or shock, actually worsened the situation and drove at least one patient's sister to slap the speaker. Among these phrases were:

- "It was God's will."

- "You'll get over it."

- "Lots of people suffer worse than this."

- "Don't look back; get on with your life."

• "Be strong for everyone else."

• "Stop crying; it just makes it harder on everybody."

• "You think that's bad, I really went through it....

Some of these phrases may seem too outrageous to be real. But I've heard each one of them and seen the devastating effect each has. Often enough, people mean well, but, as mentioned earlier, simply don't know what to say. Hence, the neighbor to the new widow: "I know how you feel; my dog just died." Sometimes it is the fear of uttering these or other awkward expressions that causes us to lapse into helpless silence.

However, the art of caring communication is eminently accessible and worthy of practice. When I was learning, my supervisors conducted practice sessions, using the technique of role playing in small groups. You might try such exercises with a friend, a parish member, or a companion with whom you may visit a nursing home, for example. If you practice role playing, you might begin with a very simple situation and improvise while you use a tape recorder to keep track of what you say. You might also try reversing roles midway, so you can get "inside" each character in the scenario.

Remember also, as we discussed last chapter, to anticipate your "hooks." When the conversation leads you to reach into your own vulnerabilities and causes you to focus on your own agenda, rather than the person you companion, remember to "put it over there on a high shelf for now."

When you practice the art of caring, you are trying to stay focused on the other person. Sometimes that is difficult; sometimes you want to turn the conversation to yourself. It is appropriate to offer sympathetic affirmation, or perhaps a brief anecdote if you've been down that particular dark alley, too. However, it is very important not to *top* the other person's pain, confusion, or problem with your own. You want to avoid trivializing what the other is feeling and show instead respect and empathy.

"I know how you feel." It is also important to be judicious with this phrase. Although it is most often well meant and compassionate, we may be shocked when it offends someone. This happens more often than most people suppose. But unless you have AIDS or cancer, unless you have been fired or divorced, to cite a few examples, you really *don't* know how the other person feels. One of my graced and gifted editors, raised in an era perhaps more gracious than ours, used to say with sincere compassion, "I haven't experienced exactly what you're going through, but I may know something of what you feel ...." This phrase held the comfort and companionship that the previous phrase missed; a phrase which could achieve the very opposite objective we seek as we practice the art of caring.

Comfort and companionship, that is what the art of caring communication is all about. I think it is true that we express this best when we do not preach, but invite the other person to think out loud with us and to feel less alone. We can companion the person in difficulty and, at the same time, respect that person's dignity and autonomy; self-perceptions which may at that moment be in shreds. In the healing stories of the gospel, Jesus almost always asked the suffering person before him, "What do you want me to do for you?"

Blind Bartimaeus said, "Lord, I want to see." I used to wonder why Jesus asked such a question since often the problem was evident, or if it wasn't, in his divinity he would certainly know the answer. Upon reflection, however, one may say that Jesus always respects our free will and gives us the opportunity to choose. We can do no less.

In this chapter, we've seen that an important aspect of the art of caring is the art of caring communication. We can indeed learn to affirm and validate another's emotions and difficulties through appropriate listening with the "eyes of the heart."

With patience and compassion we can overcome the stumbling block, "I don't know what to say, so I'd better say nothing." We can help open a person's soul to the light of caring: a reflection of "the light [that] shines in the darkness" (John 1:5), the light that the darkness cannot overcome.　　　■

<5>

The Action of Caring

Love is not love which alters when it alteration
    finds,
or bends with The remover to remove:
Oh, no! It is an ever-fixed mark...
                    — Shakespeare, Sonnet 116

Ijust want to do something."

"I just can't sit here, I want to *fix* it."

"Damn it, *someone* should be taking charge."

We know these words; we've probably even spoken them. When a problem arises, especially in our Western culture, we want to jump immediately to problem solving, to finding the Band-Aid, to "fixing" whatever it is, and we often get frustrated with a different approach.

I remember a chaplain working on my team at Sibley Hospital in Washington, D.C., a lovely man in his fifties, who had a very pragmatic approach to life. As we gathered to share the day's experiences, I was startled when Andrew slammed his fist against the table, flushed an alarming red, and said about his patients, "If I can't fix them, I don't want to deal with them."

For him, the art of listening was so difficult that it seemed an almost unendurable penance. The non-directive, empowering, eliciting approach was pure torture. "I'm not doing my job," he said over and over again. "I'm just sitting there like a piece of driftwood on a beach full of broken glass. Listening? *Empowering?* Give me a break. I'm not doing a damn thing to help anyone."

It took Andrew several months to discover that the ministry of presence, reflective listening, and open-ended questions did, in fact, help people find their own way to spiritual healing, while retaining their dignity and regaining their own power. At the beginning of his chaplaincy, Andrew had entered patient's rooms with an armload of scriptural quotes. Months later, he still referred to the Bible, but he had learned that he was, indeed, doing something when he sat in silence with a sick person or invited a family member to pray extemporaneously. More and more he was eliciting prayer from others: moving prayers, beautiful prayers, prayers from the heart, which he began to record in a notebook. This book, in turn, was passed to others, so that the fruits of listening did become a kind of "doing," though by that time, Andrew's definition of "doing" had changed.

I consider everything in the previous chapters a form of "doing" in the complex practice of the art of caring. There are, however, still more ways to make our caring tangible.

Prayer

For me, as for many caregivers, this comes first, and often comes in unexpected times and places. When I was training for chaplaincy, my supervisor suggested that I wash my hands after each patient-visit — not only for hygenic reasons, but to use that time for prayer: prayer for the person just seen, prayer for the person about to be visited, and prayer for guidance and strength for myself. Keith suggested that as I watched the water cascade over my hands that I ask that they be used as the hands of Jesus.

Keith also reminded me that before or after a difficult visit I could meditate briefly on the use of water in the sacrament of Baptism and in Christ's great mandate to wash one another's feet. I also remember other prayer times associated with water. In the kitchen of Rachel's Shelter for Homeless Women, I recall praying with my hands in a sink of dirty dishes. Other shelter volunteers use that time for prayer as well.

But prayer, of course, is not only a solitary activity; it is a wondrous bridge of connection and communion for those you seek to companion in a caring way. I have found, in my own experience, and from the experience of my gifted supervisors, that it is important not to force prayer on people who may not be ready or who may feel inhibited about praying with you.

This is a very individual thing, and we know that God hears the cry of each heart whether we draw this out into words or not. I also feel this is a very personal matter. Some people in difficulty may be in a state of denial, or anger, or bargaining (some of the stages Elizabeth Kubler-Ross outlines in her work on death and loss). They may fear any word which might break down defenses or coping mechanisms which the individual psyche desperately needs at that time.

My experience and those of others has yielded this flexible guide. At some point in a visit, perhaps not the first one, we may ask if the person would like prayer. The person may simply wish private intercessory prayer, or may want to be placed on a prayer list. Sometimes if the trust level is high enough or the situation just right, the person may welcome spoken prayer or silent prayer during your time together. It has always been my practice to ask first and respect the person's wishes.

Sometimes people will request silent prayer; often during these times, I have seen tears flow. Most often,

people have said, "Would *you* pray?" I will never forget
the Fourth of July at Sibley Hospital. I was on night
duty: the only in-house chaplain available to the entire
hospital. When my pager went off, I hurried to the wing
to which I was called.

The nurses were having difficulty with an older
woman who was due to be released the next day —
released to a family which was inconvenienced by her
presence; a sentiment that was very clear to the nursing
staff, the hospital social workers, and the patient herself.
She talked to me about this while rockets exploded over
the Smithsonian Mall and seemed dimly to punctuate the
sentences. The miniature American flags in a flower
arrangement seemed to tremble, as did the woman's
hands as they reached for mine.

We sat there in silence for a while, listening to the
fireworks. The woman's eyes were pleading; an unspoken
question was on the air. "Would you like to pray?" I
asked. She nodded, then shook her head. "You pray,
honey; just get that word up; I need it." And so I prayed
for Julia, for her family situation, and her homecoming,
and she underlined my words with small, emphatic
noises. I waited a moment to see if she wanted to add
something, as many people did at that point in prayer.
Her right hand gripped mine tighter; her left hand tugged
at my sleeve. "Tell him about my sinuses. They keep
draining. I worry about breathing...." And so I prayed for
that intention.

Again, the hand reached out and tugged at my sleeve. "Tell him about my trouble swallowing; I think it's nerves." And so I prayed for this intention and for Julia's anxiety, asking God to come into this situation and heal it. An instant of silence. This time, her hand jerked my sleeve. "Tell him about my bowel movements, honey; I haven't had one in days...." And, so, for the first time I can remember, I prayed quite specifically, at Julia's urging, for this intention, too.

We sat in prayerful silence for just a few moments. I prayed that God be with Julia through the night and during her return home. We both said, "Amen," and she put her arms up to hug me. As I turned to leave, she abruptly cried out, "Honey, honey — call the nurse! Tell her to get in here and put me on the commode. God must have sent you to me!"

Needless to say, prayer does not always produce such dramatic results, but we can never measure God's work in a human soul or in ours. This story also reminds us not only that nothing is impossible with God, but that nothing is too banal, too earthy, to be lifted into the spiritual dimension. Everything is sacred, though I think we often forget that. Jesus used spittle and mud to heal; he spoke to us through the ordinary things of life: oil and water, bread and wine. Julia taught me that night to overcome some of my own inhibitions and to learn that nothing in God's creation is beyond the realm of prayer.

The Written Word

Sometimes, even before we listen, talk, or pray, a caring approach may be made through the art of writing. I learned about the gift of brief, handwritten notes from my first mentor, Anne Barrett. Anne, whom I mentioned in Chapter Two, was my first editor. As I struggled my way through an on-deadline, massive rewrite of my first novel, I was too young, too shy, and too embarrassed by my sense of floundering, to confide in Anne right away. She was an acclaimed editor of J.R. Tolkien and other renowned authors, and was nearing the end of a stellar career.

I, by contrast, had begun my first novel as a school project and was a gawky beginner. I am not sure that I would have even entertained the thought of Anne's care for me or her companionship through a terrible struggle, if she had not dropped me all those notes. I have them still, and I shall always have them in a special box, which smells of her lavender cologne and which reminds me of how many graced teachers I have had in the art of caring.

Anne would drop quick notes to me from a museum, say, on a postcard of a beautiful painting. She would drop notes to me on stationery from a hotel next to a church we had visited together, or from the Boston athenaeum or from her endless store of unusual, beautiful, blank cards. Sometimes the note would be as brief as a sentence. Sometimes it would contain a humorous anecdote.

Sometimes it would concern itself with some question I had about "our" novel *(A Woman Called Moses).*

Always, the note said explicitly or tacitly, "I'm thinking of you; I believe in you." It was after a few months of these notes and mine back to her that I made more visits to her home in Boston and began to know her on another level, in person. Anne was a graced practitioner of the art of caring and the art of listening. She was very good at eliciting from me some confidence in myself as I thrashed through this "accidental" project. And she never made me feel foolish; she never took away my naive, shaky dignity. There was nearly a fifty-year age difference between us, but there seemed none.

And after awhile I was able, in my turn, to practice the art of caring with Anne. As we moved on to a second book and she faced retirement, I became the listener and the elicitor of confidence. Just as I had writhed through that rewrite, Anne dreaded growing old and losing her dignity. And so when I could not be in Boston with her I began collecting museum postcards and hotel stationery like hers — and I began making tangible my thoughts, my caring, my prayers for her. When she died a few years ago, all my notes were stored in a box in her apartment, just as hers are still with me.

Letter-writing and note-writing is said to be a vanishing art, but I think it is essential to the art of caring. For those of us who, like Jo mentioned in Chapter Two, feel apprehensive about how to approach someone in difficulty, a note may be preferable for several reasons.

Written communication, as discussed previously, does not put the recipient on the spot. It gives the person time to reflect and react in private. Follow-up with notes can seem less intrusive than a phone call. Finally, a note may be kept, read, and reread.

There is no reason why verbal and written communications should be mutually exclusive; in fact, they may reinforce and enrich each other. I think that an ongoing practice of note-sending is an important way to demonstrate the art of caring over a long period of time. Your words, in your handwriting, say that you still think of the person, even though a crisis is past; you are still with that person.

I like to keep a card file on hand, and I pick up interesting and attractive cards when I see them, so that all I have to do is reach for one, as needed. I regard the personally written note more helpful than a commercially written card, but those are useful, too.

The written word can be used in other forms to enact the art of caring. Just as caregivers find help in keeping journals, so too might people in difficulty, the people you companion. You might ask them if they have ever tried this, or you might present them with an attractive, blank book just as a suggestion. I have met many people who find comfort and release in writing poetry or letters about their emotions and situations. Still others find themselves companioned by books of all kinds — from novels, to self-help, to books on prayer and spirituality.

You may want to keep a few on hand as lending copies. (Two that I have found useful are *May I Hate God?* and *Good Grief,* but there are many others.) It is even more important to elicit from the troubled person what he or she likes to read, and to invite the person to share favorite books with you. The more you can encourage someone in difficulty to share, the more you empower the person to regain creative control over his or her life.

The power inherent in words resounds down through the centuries back to the primal fire, where people first began telling stories to discover who they were, where they were going, and how to heal their brokenness.

Image and Symbol

Perhaps because I have lived much of my professional life in the arts, I see great power in the arts and spirituality. The two have always been linked. For example, it is helpful for many troubled people to draw sketches of their problems or their pain from different angles. Over a period of time these sketches will change.

When I was in a training program for spiritual direction, we were all asked to draw a picture of where we felt we were at that point in our own spiritual journey. I remembered how we snorted and giggled as we reached for the pastels, "Just like kindergarten," someone muttered. At the end of the program, we were asked to make another drawing and we saw the first one, which we had almost forgotten. This exercise no longer seemed babyish or silly; it was quite stunning in what it told each of us, without words.

As we companion people in difficulty, I think we need to be alert to their gifts as well as their problems. Do they have gifts in painting? Sculpture? The feel of clay between one's fingers can be therapeutic as well as creative, and some of the greatest creations on canvas and of clay rise from personal ashes. Does the person have a gift in the area of music? Or, perhaps, the person loves and appreciates music. Music, then, can be brought in as part of the support system you facilitate around the person who is struggling. You might exchange tapes or CD's; you might attend a concert together.

And, again, most important, you may want to ask the person's advice about choices you make regarding musical purchases. If you draw on the person's strength, wherever that strength may lie, you empower him or her to do the same.

All of the arts have great power to touch and surface emotions. The dance, the theater, even mime and word play can be helpful to a person if the fit is right. And so as we listen for brokenness, we also listen for strengths and gifts, and if these gifts lie in the arts, they can be used — both for you and for the person you companion in the art of caring.

Body Work

Psychologists and doctors tell us that exercise is helpful to reduce stress, depression, and other ills. You may want to companion a troubled person simply by taking a walk with him or her. Walking is somehow conducive to thinking — and to praying. A contemplative Carmelite nun told me about "walking prayer," which she does in the monastery garden every afternoon in the time she sets aside for intercessions. There is nothing mysterious about walking prayer; it is simply that: praying while walking. It is a different experience from praying while kneeling, or sitting, or praying in community. And there is something very liberating about it.

Just as we listen for a troubled person's gifts in the arts, we might also listen for athletic gifts. The use of physical activity, sports, or the peacefulness of swimming or jogging may provide a helpful release. It may also provide you with a sense of "doing something," if you companion the person in such an activity.

There are other forms of body work in the practice of enacted caring. An important form is the area of breathing exercises. Stressed people tend to breathe quickly, which may only heighten anxiety. There are many books on breathing techniques, which calm and invigorate, just as there are many books on prayer and meditation. You and the person you companion may explore this area together. Perhaps your companion can teach you about the subject, or he or she can explore it alone. It is another way to gain a sense of momentum and a proactive stance, which may be useful after an initial time of listening, reflection, and prayer. It can be a way of getting to know each other and building trust. As we begin to be more proactive and "to do something," the foundation of listening, reflection, prayer, and emotional support is the undergirding basis for everything.

The "Little" Things

Of course, they're not so little, those little, thoughtful touches that have always helped and have become unspoken traditions. In Harper Lee's classic, *To Kill a Mockingbird,* the narrator writes, "Neighbors bring food with death and flowers with sickness and little things in between. Boo was our neighbor. He gave us two soap dolls, a broken watch and chain, a pair of good luck pennies, and our lives...."

And so we do; we bring casseroles and cakes and send flowers, but it is those "little things in between" that I'm thinking of here. What are the soap dolls and watch chains for you? For someone else?

They may take the form of a candle, a balloon, a book, bath oil, or a basket of teas, a bird house, a stained-glass sun catcher. They may be as simple as a bookmark or a napkin from someone's favorite bar and grill. Your soap doll may not be mine. My watch chain may not be a watch chain to the person I companion.

What's important, I think, about those "little things in between" is that they fit the recipient and that they help to give us, in Harper Lee's words, our lives — our lives returned to us, changed perhaps, perhaps even better. So as we listen for pain, for fear, for gifts and strengths, we also need to listen for certain clues: clues to what makes a soap doll and speaks without speaking to the very center of the person you companion in the art of enacted caring.

Ritual

"We tell ourselves stories in order to live," wrote Joan Didion in *The White Album.* And we also practice numerous rituals in order to live, from our start-the-day rituals to our closing-for-night rituals. We have rituals for life's pivotal points: deaths, births, marriages, and transitions. My spirituality has always been incarnational. And I have always found joy and comfort in such rituals as house blessings and special Masses.

Recently, a dear friend of mine was going through a series of upheavals and changes. Until her death, the most stable, loving figure in his life had been his mother, who herself had weathered many upheavals with grace and guts. She had passed to her son her love of the arts, which in turn had always steadied him in rough waters. I asked him if he would like to have a Mass said for his mother, even though she had died seven years before. His grief was assuaged, and she had had many Masses said for her. The moment I suggested this, I felt foolish. I wasn't even sure why the idea had come to mind. But my friend was pleased and touched. He put the date of the Mass on his calendar and I attended the Mass with him. He later told me that the experience had deeply moved him and put him back in touch with his strengths and his center.

Religious rituals have the combined power of word and symbol. They are important to many of us as we gather strength in order to practice the art of caring. These rituals can also be important for people in difficulty; again, we must listen carefully to discern what *they* need, rather than what *we* think they need.

There are also rituals that can be very sacred, very simple, that take place at home: a home Mass, for example, or some ritual that brings back a happy moment from long before — baking Christmas cookies in July, dying Easter eggs in January; the ritual of bedtime reading or perhaps a recreation of a long-forgotten breakfast of flapjacks and sausage.

A woman I know decided she and her husband needed a break from a period of heavy stress in their lives. She brought all the plants into the house and created a picnic, complete with checkered-cloth and wine on the living room rug, one bleak November evening. Sometimes, simply laying and lighting a fire is a ritual in itself, where the flames bring comfort, peace, and a sense of safety in a time of trouble.

You may need ritual on a regular basis, and it is my sense that we all need rituals of solace, continuity, and stability in times of crisis or distress. These rituals tend to remind us of safer times, of our centers, and of those light- bringers who lit the candles or the fire before us, so that we may rekindle our spirits again. Talking about ritual and perhaps sharing one with a person under stress is a powerful way to "do something," to enact the art of caring.

■

<6>

The Maintenance of Caring

Love's not time's fool, though rosy lips and cheeks
within his bending sickle's compass come: Love
alters not with his brief hours and weeks, but bears
it out even to the edge of doom.
　　　　— Shakespeare, Sonnet 116

The red balloon had lost its lift and lost its string. Two weeks before, at Christmas, it had proudly floated, a heart-shaped splash of color, above Thelma's wheelchair in the nursing home solarium. Now Thelma lay in another room: a room with a single bed, a room filled with the shifting hues of winter dusk, as I stood in the doorway that January. An hour earlier, I had received a call: Thelma, elderly, alone, debilitated by a stroke, had lost consciousness. The clergy from her parish could not reach her suburban nursing home this day. I could.

And so I stood there listening to Thelma's labored breathing and watching the heart balloon I had brought her move across the dim room to her bed.

What could I do here?

How could I practice the art of caring now?

I had been a parish visitor to Thelma for over a year. But this was the first time I could not talk to her — or so I thought. How could I maintain her caring presence now, when it mattered so very much?

Feeling small, I stepped into the room and felt as if I were wading into a lake. As I watched, the light turned lavender and blue and purple. Shadows gathered and abruptly I realized that Thelma was dying and dying alone. Yet somehow I felt the presence of others there. Perhaps it was the presence of those who had gone before, the presence of the saints and angels. I didn't know. I did feel the presence of Christ. And because of that presence I could approach the bed.

The heart balloon had come to Thelma before me. Flashing in the remains of the afternoon light, the shining heart hovered over her head and slowly passed down the length of her body, only to return to float just above her own heart, as if in blessing. It was a sacramental moment

112

I witnessed; yet I knew there was something more I'd been called there to do.

Thelma had lived a devout life. And somehow I sensed she needed to hear the sound of familiar prayers. I knew, too, that people in coma retain the faculty of hearing. Were my poor prayers enough? Was this piece of red Mylar enough? I put my hand on Thelma's and I talked to her. I prayed and I just sat there as the room grew dark.

The next morning, around 6:00, I dreamed that Thelma and I knelt together at communion; she touched my shoulder and smiled. She was radiant, she was whole. The phone rang in my house. It was the hospital. After I had left the nursing home, Thelma had relaxed and just moments before as I dreamed of her, she had died peacefully in her sleep. When I returned to Thelma's room to get her things, the bed was stripped and the heart balloon had ascended to the ceiling in the corner.

I remember those events when I think of practicing the art of caring long-term. I had placed limits for myself: I could show my caring only if I could speak to Thelma while she was conscious; I could pray with her only if she could look into my face. Instead, I had been called to be a witness to a quiet miracle. God's presence was with a woman who might have died alone but for that one witness, and a red balloon.

The privilege of witnessing this event taught me that the art of caring is a process, not a single event. It is not a basketball shot, a dash across a finish line, a prize won.

My last moments with Thelma were based on a year of visits and the growth of trust. I believe that in her coma, Thelma heard the voice of someone she knew. And I believe that I was able to lift my voice because I felt the presence of the One I rely upon. I also realized in a tangible, enacted way, that with God no caring act is too small.

It is my sense that we often fear the small acts. They seem insignificant to us. They seem useless; they don't seem to be enough. However, a mentor to me on the Northern Virginia Hotline reminded me, "We must have the humility to do the small things, not just the grand gestures. We must be willing to be shining chips in the mosaic of caring."

And we must be willing to believe in that mosaic if we are to maintain the art of caring as a life stance and a lifestyle. This is especially true of the countless little things we do for all those people on the inner rings of our circle of concern. These small acts create a climate of caring that opens up opportunities for more significant terms of care when the situation arises.

If we are willing, the art of caring can reposition our lives in a positive, new direction. What direction, exactly, is that?

First, one's sight is expanded to see the quiet miracles, like Thelma and her balloon's blessing. Once our eyes are opened to these miracles, we see more and more. Think of blind Bartimaeus [Mark 10] sitting by the side of the road, crying out for Jesus' mercy. This miracle story is a dramatic account of a dusty beggar, a dusty road, a crowd hushing the beggar's cries — and the blind beggar's powerful persistence.

When Jesus asks Bartimaeus what the blind man wants, the response is simple: "Lord, I want to see." *I want to see.* It is the cry of every last one of us. Once we begin to practice the art of caring we become privileged witnesses to miracles "less dramatic," but not less powerful.

A depressed friend, through the sheer power of our steadfast, loving presence, may see the light of a depression lifting. A neighbor in deep grief may see the light of life beginning again, in a new way. And we, ourselves, may see a radical new way of beholding ourselves: are we not all blind Bartimaeus? Which of us does not need a wider range of vision? *Lord, we want to see.*

As we practice the art of caring, as we witness the Thelmas and the balloons that come our way, we see more and more. We also experience a greater sense of connection and communion, even in brief moments when our lives brush others — when we stand on a threshold of a dim room with only a balloon and words of prayer for a ritual of passage.

We also find our lives repositioned in a different way. Our horizons are broadened; we are turned outward, as well as inward. Our circle of concern expands and we have a new sense of belonging to the body of Christ. The gospels ask us to reflect, "Who is our neighbor? The definition of "neighbor" in our lives grows as we practice the art of caring.

Hanging in There

We feel wonder when we witness these quiet miracles. However, when we practice the art of caring on a regular basis every experience cannot be a mountain top. How do you pace yourself so that you can maintain the art of caring on a steady basis? How do you travel through the valleys between those peaks of glory?

For example, when one first begins to practice the art of caring, there is often a sense of exhilaration which may lead us down to muddy roads. One road tempts us to take on too much; to take on every neighbor, coworker, and friend in need. This road quickly mires you down until you feel overburdened, resentful, or simply inadequate and exhausted.

Another perilous valley road is the airy, lofty path of high expectations — too high. You want to solve, to save, to fix. And when you can't, you feel disappointed in yourself, perhaps in God, and sometimes in the person you seek to help; a person whose pace of change may not be as fast as you would like. Both roads can lead to guilt, negative feelings, and a pull-back from the practice of caring.

How to cope? Here are some basic suggestions:

1. Start small.

Select one person or situation, rather than several, where you feel your presence can be helpful.

2. Define what "your helpfulness" means to you.

Do you have an affinity to senior citizens? The disabled? Someone in depression? Someone who is physically ill? It is important to be aware of your own process as you practice the art of caring and to administer from your strengths from the long-term situation before you branch out and stretch in other areas. Some people are called to companion the dying, others are called to engage a young person at risk. If you can become blind Bartimaeus for a moment, ask yourself what you need to see.

And ask God to show you where your sight is best directed. Often we experience an inner "knowing" as to where we are called into the art of caring. Other times, we are taken by surprise.

Last year, for example, I organized a project to bring free creative writing to "marginalized" people: residents of nursing homes, at-risk youth, a cancer support group. Although I have worked in all these areas, I was most drawn to the cancer support group. Perhaps my experience as a hospital chaplain contributed to this. Where are you called? When you listen in prayer, what happens? When you look into the eyes of a friend, or a neighbor, or coworker, where do you feel drawn? Sometimes it simply depends on personal chemistry, a factor which cannot be overlooked.

3. Keep your expectations reasonable.

If you set a timetable, extend it or leave it open-ended. If you expect to "save" anyone, it may be useful to think again about the image of the mosaic. "Some kind of faith life is crucial," a shelter provider once told me. "When I go home at night, I think of all these loose ends left here. That's when I need to remember that there is One who is always there after I go home, always at work in people's lives."

4. Practice "process."

The art of caring is a way of being, a lifetime process. Think of yourself as companioning a person in difficulty, rather than parachuting into his or her life like a marine. You are walking together as the disciples did on the road of Emmaus. There, too, the miracle was quiet, though awesome. The disciples only recognized their companion on the road, the risen Christ, later, as they broke bread together.

The road to Emmaus is a good paradigm for the steady, long-term practice of the art of caring. It is a journey, it is walking with a companion, *and* the Holy One. And the fruits of the journey are revealed slowly, progressively. How often the healing presence of Christ, the healing, hope-giving presence of Christ is revealed in the breaking of bread. One way to sustain your own practice of the art of caring is to anchor it to a common act: sharing food or a meal. This translates caring into action.

5. Set up a support network.

As mentioned previously, if you are companioning someone in difficulty, try to involve other caregivers to form a helping nucleus. This nucleus may comprise other friends, other coworkers, other members of various communities: church, workplace, neighborhood, and others.

Two years ago, when a close friend of mine was dying of AIDS, his friends set up a rotation system, which enabled us all to help in a way that prevented one person alone from burning out. We also enlisted the help of Meals-on-Wheels, a hospice, and a corporation which contributed assistance.

Spreading the net wide is important to prevent wearing out. It is also important on a spiritual level because it involves cooperation and community. It surrounds the troubled person with a variety of support and it guards against our own temptations, at times, to take too much control and get lured by the "power rush" that often besets caregivers, even those with the best of intentions.

6. Check with someone else.

When we seriously practice the art of caring on a long-term basis, it is important for everyone concerned to set up some checks and balances. Just as you want to find a support network, you may want to find a mentor — or at least someone with whom you can talk in confidence about the situation involving you. This person may be clergy, may be a pastoral counselor, or may simply be a person whose insight, wisdom, and discretion you trust. This person may be as close as your own spouse.

The very act of talking through a problem, of "bouncing it off" someone else, may cause you to come up with your own answers. There is great value in hearing a story told aloud, even if you are the storyteller. In the parables of Jesus, stories are presented to the crowds. After each story, Jesus asks "What do you think?" or some similar challenge or invitation. *What do you think?*

Tell the story. Ask for the response of someone you respect, perhaps someone with experience in care giving. But also listen to the story you tell as you tell it, and ask yourself what you think. Often the answers lie within you.

7. Keep a journal of your caring practice.
Make certain that this journal is marked "Confidential" and kept in a safe place. It is best to record you impressions *after* a visit or encounter. You do not want to take notes while you companion someone and thus make that person feel like "a case." You may also choose to write a verbatim, as described in Chapter Three. The act of keeping such a log can be invaluable to you as you strive to be helpful to another. However, confidentiality in this matter is absolutely crucial.

8. Develop a list of referrals.

These may be psychological, spiritual, medical, crisis intervention, and others. You will inevitably encounter situations where specialized help is needed (see "Dangers of Caring, Chapter 8). You may begin with such organizations as Alcoholics Anonymous, Meals-on-Wheels, Tough Love, and others. It is important to know how to augment your enacted caring, while remaining faithful to the person you companion. Above all, you want to portray referral as an expansion of the art of caring rather than abandonment.

9. Consider "team caring."

In every hospital there is a designated team of medical personnel on call at all times to attempt resuscitation of a dying person. Although you will probably not face this specific situation, consider forming a group of on-call support-givers. These could be half a dozen neighbors, coworkers, or friends, carefully chosen for their experience, wisdom, compassion, and *commitment.*

If someone in your parish or work place, for example, is in difficulty, you may want to mobilize a team, depending upon the nature of the situation. Such a team can meet monthly to share experience and provide support for one another. Such a team can also be in place, should an emergency arise in the workplace, the parish, the neighborhood. The team should have clearly defined levels of help.

One level might simply be food provision, i.e., a rotation of evening meal preparation, delivered to a person's home. Another level could be companioning a person in need; still another could be driving that person to the supermarket or the doctor. On a deeper level is listening and discussion of personal issues.

Again, confidentiality is crucial, as is commitment. You want to make sure you can count on team members. You also want to achieve a consensus about praying for the person who is in need. This can be done as a group, individually, or in the form of a prayer chain — or all three.

10. Build the art of caring into your schedule.
We live busy lives. Sometimes our lives are so delicately calibrated that a change in schedule threatens our sense of order, that sense of structure that seems to hold back chaos. Sit down with your weekly planner, or calendar, and see where you have "flex time" to practice the art of caring. For many people the practice comes to an abrupt halt simply because of time and commitment conflicts.

11. Build the art of caring into your spiritual landscape.
Just as we set aside flex time in our external schedules, we need spiritual support within if we are to maintain the practice of caring. You may choose to set aside prayer time each day, or every few days, for the persons you companion in difficulty. Your prayer may take many

forms: verbal, visual imagery, contemplative, individual, or communal.

You also may find it critical to set aside time to pray for God's wisdom, guidance, strength, and healing to come to you and through you. Sometimes ritual can be especially helpful. You may set aside a time each week to light a candle, and set before a crucifix the names of the people concerning you.

I know one caregiver who keeps the reproduction of a treasured icon on her wall. Under this icon, she pins the photographs of people for whom she intercedes. A spiritual director I know always tells her directees that she carries them in her heart when she receives communion.

Recently, a friend in distress reported this story. This friend had feared burdening her friends during a difficult winter. Finally she wrote to one and confided that she was going through a divorce, dealing with her mother's grave illness, and living in a new place. She felt badly about being out of touch and did not expect a reply. By return mail, she received a note with a quote from an E.E. Cummings' poem, "I carry your heart in my heart."

The loving signature was from her understanding friend. In prayer, in thought, in sacrament, through our own words and those of scripture, poets, and the saints we can carry another's heart in our heart — and we can remember that we are carried in the heart of the One who loves us most and knows us best, Jesus Christ.

To sum up:

• Start small, keep your expectations reasonable.

• Define what "your helpfulness" means to you.

• Practice caring as a "process," not a quick fix. Set up a support network involving others.

• Check in periodically with a mentor, expert, etc.

• Keep a journal of your caring practice.

• Develop a list of referrals.

• Consider "team caring," working in rotation with others.

• Build the art of caring into your schedule and calendar.

• Build the art of caring into your spiritual landscape.

There is a rhythm, a stride we hit when we maintain the practice of the art of caring. And yet we are always learning. A few years ago, I trained and facilitated a visitors' group in my parish. These visitors volunteered their time to visit the homebound, the hospitalized, and those in nursing homes. I visited parishioners and supervised other visitors, which often involved complex relation-ships and situations. We met as a group for support and further training every month. I was deeply involved with this ministry — and yet to my shock, I realized that in my own neighborhood I was missing an important current in the stream of caring.

Every other day, I would take a half hour walk around my quiet neighborhood. It was on these solitary walks, that I first met Peggy, my neighbor mentioned earlier, handicapped by severe arthritis. In order to spend time with Peggy, I had to change my carefully calibrated schedule — externally and internally. I realized how often it is easy to ignore those in our most immediate circle; those Peggys who exist in all our lives. Like the hummingbirds she loved, Peggy hovered on her porch about a year after I met her. Then after I returned from a long trip, the porch was empty. The bird feeder was empty. The house was empty. A "For Sale" sign stood on the grass. I'm grateful for the time with Peggy, and I regret the years before which were lost.

I, like blind Bartimaeus, had my sight expanded so that I could see other Peggys, other porches, other wings. Now, when I stop to talk with someone sitting on a porch, I think of Peggy with her birds as I think of Thelma with that wondrous balloon and I realize that the brush of their spirits give me strength to continue on the wondrous, sometimes wearying road we travel through the art of caring.

■

<7>

The Specialties of Caring

Atticus was right. One time he said, "You never really know a person until you stand in his shoes and walk around in them."
— Harper Lee, To Kill a Mockingbird

H i, honey — I'm positive."

Ordinarily, those words would mean "good news." Ordinarily, those words would have a kind of shine to them. But these words were spoken through the phone by Scott, a close friend for twelve years. These words, I knew, were not to announce some joyous decision, some hoped-for yes. These words were diagnostic: the results of a blood test which showed that Scott was HIV-positive. The fatal AIDS virus was in his system — and would now be a part of his life, now truncated, and a part of mine.

For the first time, when hearing bad news, I covered my eyes and thanked God that Scott couldn't see me. He was going on in a forced, bright chatter about his physician's aggressive approach, the new drugs, the cure for AIDS that was always possible. Scott had no symptoms and a strong constitution. "So don't worry, okay?" his voice danced through the phone wires.

I had no idea what to say.

Even with a comprehensive pastoral care background, I felt abruptly helpless. What could I say? "Everything will be all right?" "Oh no, how terrible?" It seemed that nothing I could say or do would be helpful; for the first time in my adult life, I was confronted with a crucial situation for which I had absolutely no preparation, no reference points, no vague guideposts. And I am not the only one.

We live in an era when any one of us may be abruptly challenged by a new situation such as AIDS or serious drug abuse. We may also be confronted by situations that always existed but were *never, never discussed* before: child abuse, spouse abuse, clinical depression, revelation of homosexuality, and others.

How do we encounter these situations among friends, neighbors, coworkers, or in ministry? Sometimes we may notice that someone is having difficulty keeping up with work, keeping up with connections, or simply seems troubled. Sometimes someone confides in us in a spontaneous burst or slowly, painfully. Other times we may notice changes in behavior, for example, missed appointments, emotional outbursts, or an inability to communicate. And occasionally someone may come to us and ask for help.

Meeting the Challenge

How do we meet these challenges as we practice the art of caring?

How do we cope with our own feelings, kicked up in us, as we try to companion someone else through foreign valleys of the shadow — strange new landscapes which may frighten us, threaten us, and even repel us, despite our best intentions?

This chapter will look at some of those special valleys: AIDS, severe depression, and suicidal behavior. Each situation is different, even from kindred areas: other terminal illnesses, grief and sadness, and desperation. Before we can companion others through these "shadow-lands," in the words of C.S. Lewis, we need a guide for ourselves. As we begin, let us return to a pair of basics in practicing the art of caring: feelings and the ministry of presence (see Chapter 3, "The Basics of Caring").

As we meet the challenges of special situations, we must stop and look within. If we're not in touch with our

emotions first, we may not be as helpful as we could be —
or we may unconsciously project our own feelings onto a
situation in a way that complicates it further. In the
cases of AIDS, depression, and potential suicide, we must
face squarely one common factor: the element of *stigma.*

No matter how open and accepting we feel, and no
matter how much societal tolerance has grown, these conditions still carry some connotations of taboo. Only
recently have we begun to discuss depression, for
example, in an open, non-stigmatizing manner. This is
especially true since the advent and publicity of the
anti-depressive medication Prozac and the many books it
has spawned.

However, only about twenty-five years ago, Senator
Thomas Eagleton of Missouri was knocked the Democratic
presidential ticket (as vice-presidential nominee), because
the press had discovered Eagleton had suffered from
clinical depression. This was a darkness one did not
speak of. It was, until recently, a topic that we locked in
the attics of our minds, as we used to literally do with
mentally ill relatives. There may still be some residue, for
all of us, from these long-prevalent attitudes.

AIDS carries a great deal of emotional freight, even in
places where this fatal auto-immune system disease is
accepted and elicits sympathy. Because AIDS is often
transmitted sexually or through IV drug use (as well as
blood transfusions), it carries connotations unlike those of
other terminal diseases. Also, because AIDS is often
associated with the gay community, another set of

attitudes may get kicked up in us as we seek to companion a person with AIDS.

Finally, the subject of suicide has always carried a frightening, threatening subtext for us. Again, it wasn't so very long ago that church and society set suicides apart in negative ways. We may carry some semi-conscious residue from older attitudes. If we do not face our internal landscapes squarely and clarify our inner terrain, we may be startled by rockslides when we least expect them. We may find a phrase or an attitude popping out in conversation — leaving us as stunned and chagrined as our listener, the one we'd hoped to help. "At least, do no harm," physicians vow in the Hippocratic Oath. And at least, *at least,* let us do none either.

When we are dealing with stigmatized, or formerly stigmatized conditions, we are dealing with human beings who not only struggle with their condition, but with fears of being *labeled, judged,* and *misunderstood.* These fears are not irrational, but grounded firmly in reality. We have heard the opinion of some that "AIDS is a punishment from God," and we have heard others demand that severely depressed people "stop being self-indulgent and pull themselves together." We have also heard suicide, enacted or contemplated, declared a sin.

Before we can walk through these shadow-lands in a helpful way to others, we must examine our own attitudes. Can we companion others without judging them? Without trying to "fix" them, or their condition?

This leads us again to the ministry of presence as a basic tool for compassionate, unconditional caring.

Often the simple act of personal acceptance is healing in and of itself — especially with someone who feels in danger of judgment, misunderstanding, or pejorative labels such as "bad" or "crazy." If we can accept each person on a case-by-case, individual basis — as a person, rather than a member of a group — we can begin to be effective.

To go further, if we can establish a relationship with the person as *a person, not a condition,* we are closer still to companioning someone in great need of a non-judgmental, accepting presence — the presence which says, as Jesus said to his disciples, "I am with you always." It is impossible to overstate this crucial factor: the person in need must be seen as a person first, a child of God, and *not* as the sum total of his or her depression, AIDS, or suicidal feelings.

We may learn to do this best, perhaps, by looking at ourselves when we feel stressed — you've quarreled with a friend, made an error at work, forgot to pick up the cleaning, gotten a traffic ticket, lost a paycheck — or any combination of such ordinary stressors. A Carmelite friend says of such times, "martyrdom by pinpricks can be very painful." True enough. We have all had such days — and perhaps, worse: days of bad news, sudden disaster, or crisis. And yet, I am not my crisis; you are not your stress. We experience stress and the inevitable life-blows, but we are not synonymous with them. Sometimes, however, we feel that we are. We have not simply *had* a failure, suddenly it feels as if we *are a* failure. A close friend who worked hard to build a business and was cheated by investors had to declare bankruptcy. It took him some years to make the discernment between that business failure and the image of *himself* as a failure. Stop and think about your own less-than-shining moments (we all have them). Are you that moment? Even if you are responsible for that moment, or partially responsible, you are not synonymous with it.

Once we grasp this truth about ourselves, it is easier to get past this stumbling block with others. They are in difficulty or are experiencing difficulties — but first and foremost each individual is a person, not a difficulty. I recall a young woman who had struggled in therapy for years over memories of childhood sexual abuse. In her adult life, she had achieved a great deal as an artist, as a friend, and as a compassionate teacher. And yet, she told her therapist, "I still feel as if I'm bad, just plain bad."

She then ran through a litany of mistakes. Her therapist looked directly at her. "How can you be bad when you think 'so good'?" he said. "You may have made mistakes — but *you* are *not* the mistake." Her self-hatred began to abate after that "curse-breaker" or breakthrough to a new understanding. If we understand ourselves this way, it is easier for us to bring this understanding to the art of caring and our "ministry of presence" with those who need to be companioned in difficult, and sometimes, special situations.

In this situation a "caring journal" can be a great help. It may be the repository for feelings in ourselves we may not like very much, but need to face, own, and deal with before we move on. Another helpful technique is a dialogue with oneself. Place the side that says, "I want to help" in conversation with the side that says, "This scares me.... I want to judge.... I want to flee."

Finally, it is important to note that we are all called to different ways of practicing the art of caring. As the apostle Paul writes in 1 Corinthian 12, Christians are given a variety of gifts and are called to a variety of missions, so that we may *all* build up the Body of Christ, in which we are one.

How do you discern if you are called to companion a person with AIDS? A person in a clinical depression? A suicidal person? How can we know if the inner voice that cries, "Flee!" is the voice of normal apprehension or a signal that we are not called to this ministry? In his fine book on Ignation discernment, Weeds Among the Wheat, Thomas Green, S.J., discusses the sense of peace that accompany a true calling.

This peace is not that of the hammock or the beach; it is the "peace that the world cannot give," the sense of unconflicted direction and rightness that goes deep, like an ocean current, unruffled by surface waves or the world's opinion. Sometimes we also experience a sense of inner compulsion to do something: a strong "I must," or a feeling of "I can't do it any longer, so help me, God." How very important it is to listen to these inner voices, perhaps to write them down, and to *remain in conversation with them* as we move forward into specific special situations in the practice of the art of caring.

The Art of Caring: People with AIDS

Perhaps you live in a community where you've seen it before: young people, often in life's prime, coping with those ironic diagnostic words: "I'm positive." Perhaps a friend's AIDS diagnosis comes as a shock. I spent a summer working with AIDS patients in a hospital, and I still remember the fresh garden flowers in the room of one burly man in his fifties. His wife, who sat with him and crocheted with trembling fingers, always brought flowers from the couple's beloved garden, around the corner. Her husband had contracted the AIDS virus through a blood transfusion during surgery a few years before.

However AIDS is contracted, it presents a sense of helplessness to those of us who would be a caring companion. Sometimes we come up against sexual baggage: our own feelings, perhaps biases. Sometimes, we hit the sense of tragic injustice of a contaminated blood transfusion and find ourselves thrown, as if against a stone wall, against our own inner questions about how a loving God can allow such suffering, a mystery as old as theology itself. One thing you can be sure of: you will be asked for answers to the unanswerable — "Why me?" "How could this happen?" "Why did Go...?"

And if you try to provide answers, it is my experience that you will feel even more helpless, or perhaps inadvertently complicate the caring companionship you seek to provide. With AIDS, especially, when the outcome, thus far, is fatal, and sufferers often feel stigmatized, it is especially important to avoid trivializing the situation or presenting cheery "solutions," which always ring false. I have been told this by people with AIDS themselves.

In the case of my close friend, who died at thirty-five of AIDS complications, the most helpful things I could do were listen with compassion and acceptance to his spectrum of feelings (from anger to depression to isolation to a jaunty defiance), and state no solutions but offer a stance of solidarity: "I care; I'm with you." We may feel such phrases are so very inadequate; they may sound tinny and small in our own ears. But they represent what we *can* give, in the face of the insoluble: quite simply, ourselves, our presence and our unconditional acceptance, which are crucial to all who suffer, especially those who feel stigmatized by their condition.

Jesus did not tell us we would not suffer; he did, however, promise to be with us till the end of time. If we can become icons of Jesus, Emmanuel, God-with-us, we can mediate God's presence to someone who may feel utterly abandoned by the One who loves and knows us best. And that, in the final analysis, is no small thing.

In the other special situations that follow, we will see how flexible and powerful this stance is, no matter how disparate the various areas it touches.

The Art of Caring: Depression

This is the third time she's called to cancel a lunch date. When you finally go to visit her, your neighbor's eyes are dull. Her usually shiny hair is lank, and she has no appetite for the home baked bread and tea you bring her. She lies in the darkened bedroom, long past noon. She's been waking up very early in the mornings, she says, but at night she can't sleep. It is hard to get out of bed in the morning. As you talk further, you sense that she has lost interest in just about everything, and feels passive, helpless, and unspeakably sad. You sip your tea, puzzled. Your neighbor's life has not changed and, in fact, seems to be a good one. What caused this?

As you continue to listen she says that these "low spells" have come before, just; this is the first time she has told anyone.

"My husband says, 'Just get up and take a walk. Get out of the house; go shopping. I'd feel depressed, too, if I laid in a dark room all morning.' " Your neighbor smiles wanly. "He doesn't seem to get it." She closes her eyes.

And you, holding your tea cup wondering what to say, do *you* get it?

Recently, clinical depression has become more widely recognized and discussed than ever before. It has, in a sense, been let out of the attic. And yet, there is a lingering stigma around depression and people who suffer from it. On some level, depression congers in us frightening images of the mentally ill; Brontes' Mrs. Rochester in her attic, Dickens' Miss Haversham wandering through her dark house, Vincent van Gogh's self-mutilation.

Today, clinical depression may be recognized as an illness, a result of brain chemistry rather than "weakness "self-indulgence, or an inability to cope. Even so, many people who suffer with depression still report a sense of shame, stigma, and feeling misunderstood. I recall a depressed person whom I counseled who said, "I feel as if I'm at the bottom of a well. Faces appear at the rim, words drop down to me, but no one knows what it's like down here. Even if they *say* they do." A sense of isolation, stigma, and misunderstanding only further deepen and darken that well. As we practice the art of caring with depressed people, we must learn how to companion them in that darkness and how to recognize its signs.

Many symptoms of depression were mentioned above, and for you, the caregiver, it is important to know what they are. It is also important to listen closely for indications for suicidal thoughts (which will be treated in the next section).

Depression takes more than one form. *Reactive depression* is, as its name implies, a reaction to an event or events, which produce disappointment, grief, and anger. It is often turned inward. Many psychologists have stated that much of reactive depression is, indeed, anger turned within. For example, your company downsizes and you are summarily fired. You feel angry that your anger has no defined target. And, in any event, there's nothing you can do about it.

On some level, though, you may blame yourself: "I could have done a better job. Maybe it was me after all." Or you could experience that "Why me?" sense of unanswerable frustration. Perhaps a dream has died, or a person, or a time in your life.... Perhaps a relationship has died and you have "gotten over it" on a cerebral level; you try to "get on with your life," without giving your feelings a chance to surface. These are some of the causes for reactive depression, which may respond to counseling, to recognition of the emotions, and, of course, to the ministry of presence from you as you companion the depressed person.

Clinical depression, by contrast, seems to be rooted more in physiology or brain chemistry. It responds to a variety of anti-depressant medications, as well as therapies of different sorts. Another, often hidden cause for depression, can be other kinds of chemical imbalances, for example, low blood sugar or hypoglycemia. This condition, the opposite of diabetes, is caused by an overproduction of insulin, which causes weakness, and quite often a drop in mood, a sense of "crashing," which all of us experience when we go too long without eating.

Depression takes on many forms with many causes, and yet it presents us with the same face: the mask of tragedy. We see it as half of the emblem for the drama. It is as old as the ancient Greeks who recognized and portrayed it.

Your knowledge of depression will help you understand why your neighbor in the darkened room cannot feel better simply by "getting out of the house." Although exercise helps all forms of depression, quite often a seriously depressed person cannot at first address the simplest things: paying bills, cooking supper, walking around the block. It is in this phase that the practice of the art of caring can be the most useful. To the person at the well's bottom, to the person lying in the darkened room, a sense of acceptance and understanding is absolutely crucial.

In this situation, as in the above, there are words that help and words that wound. The depressed person probably feels guilty or ashamed as it is. You certainly will not alleviate those feelings with such phrases as: "Just pull yourself together," "Get up and do something," or, "Try to think of others."

This is not about selfishness. Once we grasp that concept we can be much more effective in practicing in the art of caring with depressed people.

In order to go the distance in this practice we must come to terms with another fact: working with depression may be a long process. Depression often takes the form of a spiral, just as grief does, where the person may begin circling her or his way out of the well, only to hit a setback. We must be prepared to deal with our own lack of patience in this art of caring. Remember, depressed persons are on their own timetables, not ours, not the timetables we *think* they should follow.

There are certain measures we may encourage, such as professional counseling. However, it is my feeling that this subject should not be broached immediately unless the situation is life-threatening, but should come after a certain level of trust has been established. The depressed person may not see your suggestion of counseling as helpful if you say, "I really can't help you. I think you need to see someone." The depressed person may hear that as a rejection, may see that as a giant step backwards, even as an act of revulsion on your part.

When you reach the point where you feel it would be helpful to suggest counseling, it would also be helpful to suggest that you help find a therapist and accompany the depressed person for the first visit. It is also important to emphasize that you will continue to be there for the depressed person; the therapist is not a substitute for your companionship and support.

What else can you do as you stand at the rim of the well and listen to the person at the bottom? As always, you can do just that: simply listen. The depressed person often needs desperately to be heard and understood. Phrases may begin as, "This may sound crazy but...." Often, however, externalizing the feelings in the form of words is a healing work, especially when there is a witness. Again, as with AIDS, we need to take on the non-judgmental, accepting stance that is so powerful in the ministry of presence.

This is not the time for problem-solving; this is not the time for quick solutions. In many cases, those solutions lie within the person. So many depressed people have told me how pressured, how rushed, and how "blown-off" and dismissed they feel when a listener immediately jumps into a problem-solving mode. Before external solutions are addressed, the depressed person needs a witness, a companion, someone who demonstrates acceptance of the other's darkness; the reality of the "well."

Over and over, I've heard depressed people almost cry, "I *just want someone to hear me out.*" And not just once. In depression particularly, follow-up is important. A depressed person who confides in you may fear turning you off; you want to show that this isn't the case. Sometimes a note, a phone message, or a flower can also augment your ministry of presence.

Recently, a depressed woman, feeling isolated, received a card in the mail which followed up on a concerned phone call. The caller was a member of this woman's parish, a friendly acquaintance. The expression of concern by phone, then by card, and then by another phone conversation did a great deal to lift the depressed woman's spirits. Her sister-parishioner wrote on the card, "Our God is often silent and when he writes, he writes in the sand." This was accompanied by the poem "Footprints," about Jesus' carrying us across the desert, even when we feel alone.

Although the depressed woman had heard that story often, it was given new meaning by her friend's nonjudgmental caring and follow-up. When the caregiver in this case was thanked, she said, "These cards seem so small, but I'm startling to think the small things are the big things when it comes to the Spirit. At least I hope so." This parishioner, a eucharistic minister, also gave her depressed "sister" respect by refusing to pressure her. Unsaid was the pointed and oft-quoted, "We *missed you* in church. Will you be there next Sunday?" The caregiving parishioner allowed the other to go at her own pace, which actually accelerated. "I didn't have to resist anything," the depressed woman told me later. "I just felt totally accepted. And through my friend's accepting care, I began to feel accepted again by God."

In the healing stories of the gospels, we may note that Jesus does not pass judgment on those who come to him in suffering. And in the parable of the Good Samaritan (Luke 10:25-37) while upstanding community members walk by the sufferer, the Samaritan (an ethnic enemy) takes the sufferer to an inn, sees to his care, and pays for it. We cannot walk by if we are to live the gospel, but can we always stay, long-term, at the inn for the whole recovery? Often we cannot. And this is not always advisable; it isn't helpful to make another dependent upon us.

Another question that often arises with depressed persons deals with the "circle effect." You may notice a circularity to the depressed person's talk, and a lack of resolution. After several "circular" talks, the caregiver may lose patience and, despite all best intentions, begin to see the depressed person as self-indulgent.

Because working through depression is a long process, it is important to spread the support network wider — to have an innkeeper as in the Good Samaritan, and others to help while you, like the Samaritan, must be about your other business. And as mentioned above, counseling and other treatment must be suggested, *not* as a substitute for your caring presence, but as an addition to it.

Other helpful practices might be journal-keeping for you and the depressed person or discussion of the Psalms of Lamentation, in which the sufferer cries out to God in pain, as in Psalm 28 ("To you, 0 Lord, I call; my rock"), and Psalm 22, from which Jesus' cry of dereliction from the cross is derived ("My God, my God, why have you forsaken me?"). In my experience as a chaplain, discussion of Psalm 22 and of Jesus's cry from the cross were extremely helpful for people who were suffering deep depression, as well as terminal illness.

Another helpful psalm is Psalm 139, beginning, "0 Lord, you have searched me and known me...," especially verses 9 through 10, "If I take the wings of the morning and settle at the farthest limits of the sea, even there your hand shall lead me...." This psalm is especially consoling to those who feel isolated in their depression and are not ready to be rushed into psalms of comfort, such as the beloved Psalm 23.

If — and only if — the depressed person feels so disposed, you might encourage that person to annotate the psalms with his or her own feelings, to write a personal psalm of lament, or pray the psalms aloud. However, many depressed people will not feel ready for this step, and until they do should not be forced. But some sort of external expression of the feelings is helpful: stream-of-conscious-ness writing or free-writing. Drawing the depression and/or the depressed person with pastels is another technique I've found very helpful.

It worked very well for a graced and gifted Carmelite nun, who has been my friend for twenty years. In her mid-forties she became clinically depressed. No matter how she tried, she could not combat the depression; she only sank deeper into it. Desperate, she went to her prioress who told her to pray more, and develop more than what seemed "impoverished faith." My friend, a very devout sister, got worse; now in addition to her depression, she experienced dangerous self-condemnation. Finally, she sought permission to visit another Carmelite monastery where there was a sister who was also a psychiatrist.

She stayed about three months as a guest at the other monastery, where she received both spiritual direction and psychiatric help from Sister Deseree. In addition to listening, praying, and talking together, my friend was asked to make a series of drawings of what she called the "grayness in me." Gradually, in her drawings, the grayness began to move outside of her. She was also eventually helped by medication.

Finally, she returned to her own monastery and has since been elected prioress more than once. She has contributed vitally to her community's life, sits on the council, and feels closer than ever to God, to Gethsemane, and to Christ's passion. She has been able to help other sisters in depression as, she says, she could not have before her own "walk through the valley of the shadow."

The most crucial thing to her recovery, she feels, was the fact that she was companioned in this valley. She adds that, although nothing has the same impact as human caring, she also felt companioned in her depression by the music she listened to on headphones and by the flowers, both in the monastery garden and those placed by caring sisters in her room.

The arts and simple beauty can often widen the rim of depression's dark well. As people begin to move up a bit from the well's bottom, it may help them to make a daily list of a very few, small, manageable activities, such as filling a bird feeder, watering the plants, walking for ten minutes, reading a poem, writing a page in a journal, sending a note. As depressed people experience a little bit more momentum in their situations, they may want to choose something they can do for someone else.

For example, I knew a depressed person who experienced a strong sense of uselessness. Among the many factors that helped him was baking a weekly pan of brownies and sending it to a homeless shelter. Grateful notes came back to him. "I'm doing something," he said to me in surprise. "I'm actually doing something." The size of the "something" never matters in the art of caring.

The Art of Caring: Suicidal Behavior

For two years, I worked a regular shift on the Northern Virginia Hotline. One Saturday night, I took a call from a narcotics officer, a seventeen-year veteran of the police department. Tough, seasoned, and experienced, this man had reached his breaking point. Abruptly, to his own surprise, he had come up against that one case which was too much. This night, working without his partner (who was ill), the police officer had found in an alley a f fifteen-year old girl, dead of a heroin overdose. The syringe and needle protruded from her right eye; she had run out veins and had injected her retina.

I spent my entire shift listening to this caller — to his pain, frustration, anger, and grief. He felt useless, and intermittently he felt suicidal. All through the night, he stayed on the phone with the hotline; passed along from shift to shift, he made it to daylight, when he could talk with the partner he so missed. But that was not enough.

In the log we kept for suicidal cases, I followed a string of calls the officer made to the hotline over a period of months. It took him that much time and that many calls to work through his suicidal feelings, raised by one night's tragedy which stood for him as a symbol of his sense of failure, worthlessness, and hopelessness about his own life.

On the hotline we had been carefully trained to listen for certain signs of suicidal feelings: that deadly trio of worthlessness, helplessness, and utter hopelessness. These feelings, combined with isolation and a lack of hope, goals, or plans, make the situation still more ominous. If the person does not feel a desire to go on, and expresses that, we were told to regard such talk as extremely serious — disregarding the popular misconception that "those who talk about it don't do it."

In fact, any time someone speaks about ending his or her life those words should not be seen as "crying wolf." Even though the threat *can* sometimes be used in a manipulative way, the fact that suicide is on a person's mind at all cannot be taken lightly.

Furthermore, if a person with suicidal feelings has a plan and the means at hand to carry out the act, more active intervention is necessary. To recap, it is important to listen for the following: feelings of hopelessness, help-lessness, and worthlessness; isolation; an absence of future- oriented thinking; and a specific suicide plan and the means to carry it out.

It is also important to remember that suicidal feelings tend to ebb and flow. On the hotline, we were trained to keep a suicidal person talking in the hopes that the intensity of his or her feelings might lessen; another reason was to give us time, if necessary, to trace the call and send the rescue squad or police.

As you practice the art of caring, and as you companion people through such life-crises as divorce, bereavement, job-loss, depression, illness, and other situations, it is important for you to know how to listen for signs of suicidal behavior. These may pop up suddenly and may pass by easily if you don't know how to recognize them or what to look for. If you are prepared for these signs, they will not seem as threatening to you and you will feel less helpless in the face of them.

Divorce, bereavement, job loss, etc., may not at first seem to warrant suicidal responses. However, as Harper Lee writes in the classic *To Kill a Mockingbird,* you never really know a person until you get inside him or her and see the world from his or her point of view. This kind of empathy is not restricted to saints and poets. We can, if we wish to, cultivate it in ourselves. I have seen two families completely stricken by a job loss. I have seen husbands so paralyzed, they cannot even begin a new job search, while their self-esteem plummets to dangerous lows. I have seen their wives working so hard that resentment builds and the whole family system begins to unravel. In this era of downsizing and furloughs, we need to be especially sensitive to the devastation of job loss and its ripple effect.

Divorce and bereavement, of course, are highly stressful, life-changing situations, which may also involve guilt as well as great pain. I have known friends, neighbors, and coworkers who have gone through divorces — and you have too. Again, it is extremely important to react with sensitivity to such events. However you may feel about the subject of divorce, or the individual situation, it is crucial to remember that, above all, the person involved is a human being in pain.

Sometimes others will pull back and subtly withdraw support in these situations. Other times people may make judgmental statements in the guise of "advice." I think this is a time when we need to focus on the individual's pain and sense of loss; the world seems to turn upside down. It is always my prayer that I may companion the person on this level and leave judgment aside. I have also noticed that I can be fooled by a person's outward appearance: what Carl Jung calls "the persona." Someone may appear perfect, especially someone I'm used to perceiving as accomplished and in charge. It is always crucial to look behind the mask, without being intrusive. We need to remember that even those who appear to "have it all together" suffer too.

I would like to add another note here. Crisis can sometimes occur even in the midst of a positive event, e.g., marriage, remarriage, moving, a new job, or a new baby. Sometimes in these situations our sensitivity level may drop. "Isn't this great," we think. "What's the problem?"

And yet these wonderful events *can* bring problems. Each one of the above situations is destabilizing and changes one's life-dynamics. For example, a major move from one location to another involves loss, stress, and change. The same thing may be true with a new job. A counseling professor taught me about a syndrome called "success-depression," in which the person who reaches the pinnacle suddenly feels a crash, a drastic letdown after striving so hard. In other cases, some people fear they will not be able to live up to new expectations and begin to doubt their self-worth as never before.

A marriage or an addition to the family changes an entire family structure and, again, involves loss: the loss of the familiar, the loss of old patterns, and the addition of new challenges. At such times, psychologically, suppressed emotional baggage often surfaces. It is important to keep these factors in mind as we companion people in joy as well as in sorrow.

The subject of remarriage is a good case in point. Again, whatever our feelings may be about the new marriage, we must remember that the people involved are making a drastic change which reshuffles their deck of life's cards. These people probably have already gone through a protracted form of suffering, either through bereavement or divorce. The new couple knows the price of a happy marriage far better than a first-time bride and groom in their twenties. And the new couple probably needs even more emotional support because they bring more experience with pain and longing, and they bring tremendous hope for what may seem "their last chance to be happy."

I have witnessed unfortunate comments regarding new couples: instead of "I'm so happy for you," or "I wish you the best," I have heard, "How'd you get divorced so fast?" or "How'd you get an annulment so fast?" or "How very difficult this must be for your former spouse." New marriages are like new jobs, new homes, new babies. All require nurturing, sensitivity, and our caring presence.

We have looked at various life crises in which we are
called to care, and highlighted some of the difficulties
these situations present. The skills learned in this book
can be applied to them all. But what if these crises lead
us to that dangerous ground, touched on earlier: signs of
suicidal behavior?

Once you notice suicidal signs, what do you do? How
do you companion someone through this darkest valley
where you yourself may feel helpless? That night on the
hotline I would have felt totally helpless if not for my
training. The policeman I spoke with was calling from a
pay-phone because he did not want to betray what he
perceived as "weakness" to his fellow officers. When he
called, his trusted partner was not available to listen to
him. He had a loaded service revolver with him as he
talked to me. All I could do was listen, validate his
feelings, bear his anger ("You people just don't know what
it's like out here — damn it, you just don't know"), and
keep him talking. I tried to reflect back to him the
feelings I heard, and I tried to meet him on a "feeling
level." Instead of getting into a cerebral discussion of
drugs, I tried to stay focused on this man's rage and sense
of personal uselessness. He wept, he roared, he swore,
and through that long night, five hotline shifts stuck with
him. To me, sticking with a suicidal person is perhaps the
cardinal principle.

This returns us again to the ministry of presence —
the sheer power of being fully present to another human
being — no matter what. Somewhere during that night,

a policeman's feelings shifted away from suicide simply because he had not been abandoned, which was precisely what he had expected.

Although his suicidal feelings returned, he did not act on them. He talked them through repeatedly until months later he was able to resolve them. In his first few weeks of calls, he was not ready for problem solving, for finding answers. He needed to writhe in the agony of long-suppressed feelings and long-ignored questions — and in this he desperately needed to be companioned; he even said so.

At a certain point, it is also helpful to explore the person's connections to the world: Who will miss him? What will be left unfinished? Sometimes, sadly, people have told me that they are alone and *no one* would miss them. Sometimes there is an undergirding motive for suicidal thoughts: a subconscious or semi-conscious desire to use death as revenge or a drastic expression of anger.

These questions are best explored with a professional counselor, and in all protracted cases of suicidal thoughts or behavior, a professional should be brought into the picture — not as a substitute for your support, but to enhance it.

Sometimes when people are at rock-bottom, isolated, and cannot see a future, you can encourage them, for the short term, simply to postpone suicide. I remember a young, pretty teacher whose students adored her. Little did they know that memories of the past echoed through her mind and her present personal life had left her feeling broken inside. She manifested all the warning signs but a skilled friend was able to get her to wait until the semester's end for the sake of her students. By the end of the semester, the teacher had begun work in therapy, had improved her personal life, and was grateful for her life and its future. Many cases may be less dramatic, but encouraging someone to postpone suicide may be a vital step toward healing.

Even with the best of intentions, if you provoke guilt in the suicidal person, you may achieve undesirable effects. For example, caregivers may say: "What about your mother? How could you do that to her?" or "What about that unfinished work? Aren't you being selfish?"

However true, such words may only deepen the worthlessness the suicidal person already experiences, and exacerbate the situation. In addition, using God's name in a guilt-producing way may increase the suicidal person's despair. This person needs to feel not God's wrath but God's presence — that radical non-abandoning presence called in the Old Testament *chesed,* a word which means "steadfast love."

A suicidal person may be able to hold on to God in the dark, but not always. In most cases, the suicidal person needs to feel God holding on, never letting go. This is often demonstrated best through you as an icon of God's loving presence, rather than by preaching. It is what Mother Teresa calls, "preaching without preaching, by the catching force." Suicidal people may also feel a sense of stigma and sense of shame about the very feelings they experience, feelings which have been stigmatized in the past.

If suicidal people are open or desirous of any scriptural comfort, I have found these two passages most useful: Jesus in the garden of Gethsemane, and the parable of the shepherd who leaves the ninety-nine to seek the one who is lost, and who brings back that missing one in triumph on his shoulders. I have seen this second story bring people to tears — freeing, cleansing, cathartic tears which open up and release frozen feelings and buried hope once again.

Suicidal situations are among the most challenging ones we face as we practice the art of caring. We, ourselves, need support in such situations. We need to talk about the situation, seek advice, or write our feelings down in a private journal; confidentiality, in all cases, is absolutely crucial. If we seek a mentor, it must be a trusted one, who will respect privileged, utterly private communication. It is also invaluable to involve others to spread the network wider without necessarily mentioning the word "suicidal."

I was profoundly grateful for my shift partners and colleagues on the hotline as I worked with the suicidal police officer. Sometimes, however, there is a temptation to take everything on one's self. In a variety of pastoral care situations, we must remember the importance of our willingness, as caregivers, to be a part of the mosaic, a shining chip of stone in the glorious, grand design.

■

<8>

The Dangers of Caring

Two roads diverged in a yellow wood and sorry I could not travel both and be one traveler.
— Robert Frost

Dangerous?

The art of *caring*?

Isn't this one of those *good* things that makes you and everyone else feel just that: *good*? How could there possibly be any pitfalls in a helping, care-giving process?

Sometimes we don't like to recognize such pitfalls, even as we fall directly into them. Sometimes we don't like to talk about them or deal with them in any conscious way. However, to sustain the practice of the art of caring, it is vital to know where the road steepens and where the turns may lie.

The Dangers of Caring:
Getting Involved, Getting Hurt?

This is one of the classic dilemmas of the helping professions. If you become involved with someone who is in difficulty and if you have empathy, you may indeed open yourself up to suffering along with that person. My father, a dedicated surgeon, used to talk about the healer's dilemma: to remain emotionally detached from the patient while doing a good clinical job, or to become emotionally involved with the patient and run the risk of suffering if you happen to lose that patient.

The first way may be the simpler way and the more self-protective way. Its proponents suggest that a physician, for example, may be more effective if he or she is less emotionally involved with the patient. And it is a commonplace that physicians never operate on their family or close friends. My father, however, chose the second way and was well-aware of the cost. It was a conscious decision, an intentional decision he made and it was the only way he could practice medicine. To him, anything less was not fulfilling his calling.

Perhaps my father's choice was influenced by a formative crisis in his childhood. He grew up as a poor, white kid in a multi-racial, multi-ethnic slum in what is now Harlem. Around the age of seven, he developed blood poisoning in his lower right arm from a puncture wound in his hand. There was no family doctor; his shopkeeper parents were too poor.

At the clinic where he was finally taken, the attending physician decided that the boy must suffer the amputation of his arm in order to save his life before the blood poisoning became systemic. However, another doctor was brought in to consult. This doctor took a look at the thin-faced intense boy and decided to give the arm "a chance," in my father's words. The arm was saved during a protracted illness, and my father emerged from the ordeal with a clear resolution to become a surgeon himself.

In fact, he did and became chief of surgery at Harlem Hospital. His patients were often those who could not pay, and I recall many silent dinners, when my father would sit brooding, at the end of the table. Occasionally I would ask him if something was wrong. "I've got some sick people in the hospital," he would ever say.

Perhaps he paid too high a cost by empathizing so deeply with his patients. Perhaps his emotional dedication took a dangerous toll on his relationships with wife and daughter. But in the end, I know that the rewards he felt, even in the sharing of pain, the sharing of sorrow, far outweighed the emotional cost for him. And

159

his empathy never interfered with his highly regarded performance as a master surgeon.

In my own life, perhaps because of this role model, I have always erred on the side of compassion, rather than clinical distance. Again, for me, this was a conscious choice and a function of my personality. Unlike my father, I was completely unscientific, highly artistic, and spiritual. And, yet, in our different ways, we both chose to get emotionally involved and pay the price of shared pain, as well as shared joy with those we have, so differently, companioned. In fact, for me, and I suspect for my father, the sharing of the pain is an important part of the journey we make with others. I wonder if there can be as much joy in the recovery or renewal of another person if we have not also suffered with them.

However, it is very critical to be aware of this cost at the outset. It is also important to take certain precautions. I think it is essential for caregivers to have a caring support system themselves: people to whom they can confide, with whom they can weep, "ventilate" emotion, and generally "be real."

My father, who grew up in a less psychologically oriented age, kept everything inside, and this, in turn, took an unnecessary toll on his own health, emotional and physical, and on his family. When we care for others beyond our families, in our immediate circle of friends, coworkers, or neighbors, we must take care to not exclude or emotionally abandon those closest to us.

A husband, wife, or close friend, for example, can often feel shut out from one's pastoral care activities, as I noticed when I studied in seminary myself. I could see and feel the pull of all those needy people, and I could see how after a certain point I could deceive myself into thinking they needed me more than other people in my life did. This is a temptation to guard against; a siren call for which to listen.

The fact is, none of us is completely indispensable. People in helping professions are always warned against "savior complexes," which delude us into thinking that we have more power to "save" the troubled, or the lost, or the suffering than we actually do. This attitude, in turn, becomes a kind of egotism, a sort of insidious, tricky pride. Some people are attracted to the helping professions because they need to feel needed, and it is important to examine, over and over again, in prayer and reflection, what our true motivation is in each case.

It is possible to strike a balance — to get involved with someone else's pain in an empathic way while at the same time including your most intimate circle in the experience. Confidentiality must be strictly respected, and my father, as I recall, took his Hippocratic Oath very seriously. But there is a way of discussing our caring involvements without revealing names or identities and sharing, at least, the emotional content with our intimate, "significant others," rather than shutting them out.

Sometimes it happens that those closest to us begin to get involved themselves in the art of caring and become

161

companions on the way. Others, quite frankly, may say such things as, "Where do you find these people? Why do you get so *wrapped up* in these people; what do they have to do with you, really?"

Such words may veil a fear on the other person's part, a fear of losing you, your full attention, or your commit-mended to them. Such statements may also cover a sense of guilt in the person who secretly feels he or she "should be doing something," but who isn't ready or able to do any-thing at this time. My feeling is this: as painful as it is to hear such pronouncements, I think it is best for all concerned to take a breath and refuse to be hooked into self-defense, argument, and, perhaps, counter-accusa-tions.

However, I feel it is equally important, even crucial, for you to find some supportive companions who will listen to you, understand what you are doing, and give you encouragement in those times of exhaustion *and* elation, failure *and* freedom. There are also other ways, which we'll discuss in this chapter, of finding the emotional support we need if we are to avoid some of the traps and pitfalls we encounter as we walk the long road. This is the pilgrimage we make as we practice the art of caring.

Mentors and Guides

In the various forms of pastoral work I've done, I have had gifted, wise supervisors or mentors. They have taught me, they have answered questions, they were there to talk to us at the hospital when a member of the chaplain team went through a failed Code Blue (resuscitation attempt of a dying person), or a patient's death. In the shelters, I remember the "kitchen conferences" I had with Sr. Mary Ann who directed Rachel's Shelter for Homeless Women, conversations which clarified issues for me and which also provided me with camaraderie and support.

In nursing homes, there were social workers who often illuminated particular cases for me, and in the D.C. jail, every day began with simple prayer, a reminder by the head chaplain, a seasoned, humorous, humble priest, that we were not there to judge. Throughout each chaotic day he was there to answer questions, provide a needed laugh, and put situations in perspective.

However, for most of us who are practicing the art of caring in our immediate circle, there are no supervisors or the like. We must find others — spiritual directors, wise friends, perhaps a spouse, or someone experienced in the field with whom we can meet regularly or call when we need guidance. We need people like that in this caring practice which has no easy recipes or formulas, but which opens us to surprise and grace and gift.

Mentors can also help us do "reality-testing," if we are not sure that we are choosing to handle a situation well or speaking the words that will help rather than harm.

As you begin to expand your own practice of the art of caring, I strongly suggest that you seek out a spiritual director, a good and trustworthy friend or family member, or someone experienced in counseling. Ask this person if he or she might be willing to listen to you from time to time and consult with you as you face new bends and turns on this road you have chosen.

In certain situations, such as suicidal behavior or alcoholism, such consultation is essential. It does not mean that you have failed, that you "can't handle it," or that you are abandoning the person in stress whom you have companioned. It simply means that you are trying to provide the greatest, richest kind of caring support for someone in need — and for yourself, to enable you *both* to go on.

When to Refer

When do we make the suggestion that a suffering person see a professional?

Never? Immediately? Routinely? Life or death situations only?

Or, perhaps, though we make cringe to admit it, we refer people when we are fed up, exhausted, or scared. Unfortunately, there are no recipes or formulas that are foolproof in every situation. This is an art, not a science. And although this may make it harder, I am grateful for that. I am grateful that each individual situation is different and pulls on different parts of our own humanity.

I think we must approach the issue of referral on a case- by-case basis and always with great care. It is crucially important that the person you companion feel abandoned or rejected if you refer them to a professional. It is equally important that they do not interpret the referral as a big stamp of disapproval, "certifiable behavior," or a stigma. If referral is done without sensitivity and continuity from you, all of these emotions may rise in the person you seek to help. Moreover, that person may react so adversely that the referral will not be taken.

Whatever the situation, the referral should be presented as an additional form of help and support, and *never* as a substitute for yours. Suppose you no longer feel adequate to help a coworker with severe clinical depression. You may ask your colleague how he or she might feel about talking to someone *in addition* to you and explore those feelings before making any moves.

Even in this psychologically-oriented age, some people still feel stigmatized by seeing a therapist. Others, unfamiliar with the process, may imagine it as threatening, blaming, or accusatory. Still others may fear what a therapist might unearth. It is helpful to talk this through with the person you companion, validate and honor his or her feelings without judging them, and perhaps share some of your own experiences with therapy of others.

You cannot make an appointment for another person with a therapist; the person must do that for himself or herself. And you must be prepared for a time of vacillation and reflection before the person may be ready to do it. It can be extremely destructive to place conditions such as the following on this decision:

- "I'm not going to put up with this if you don't get help."

- "Fine, but don't expect me to keep listening to this."

- "I've tried, God knows I've tried, and if you won't get help, there's nothing else I can do."

- "I'm just enabling you to stay in this bad situation, so get help or that's it for me."

- "Do you want to go on this way and ruin everybody's lives? Then you'd better get help."

- "I refuse to be codependent any more. From now on, it's your problem."

I have heard all of these lines spoken more than once by exhausted caregivers, family, and friends. We are not addressing here the complex dynamics of family systems. But we are certainly addressing a real dilemma for caregivers moving among the concentric circles of friends, neighbors, and coworkers. As you can see these statements are all threats, to different degrees.

Instead of enabling and empowering a person to seek extra help, these words attempt to motivate by fear. I have seldom seen them achieve much, although on the surface, such ultimatums may have gotten people into counseling for a brief period of time.

Some caregivers believe that certain situations warrant such absolute pronouncements, especially in the case of alcoholism or substance abuse. When I studied the art of ministering to alcoholics and their families, I was blessed with an exceptional teacher, a recovering alcoholic who ran a treatment center with his wife, also a recovering alcoholic. It was his feeling that "an intervention" by family or close friends could be made in an alcoholic's life or alcoholic situation even before the alcoholic "hit bottom."

This teacher's methods for the complex process of an intervention, however, never involved conditions or threats. Instead, they were predicated on love, concern, and belief in the individual's inherent capacity for wholeness. One of the key lines this teacher suggested was quite simple, and I have known several instances in which it has proven highly effective. A member of my chaplaincy team, in fact, used this method with his own father. He and his brothers had packed a bag, reserved a place in a good treatment center, and sat down with their father one evening.

Holding the alcoholic father's hands, Patrick said with tears in his eyes, "Pop, this just isn't you; this isn't the you I remember; this isn't the you that even you, yourself, remembers. We want you back. We miss you. We love you. We're with you. Please go to this place, so that the real you can come back." The father, his own face streaming with tears, picked up his suitcase and went for treatment. He has been sober ever since. Part of his sobriety is due to the fact that he was not threatened or shamed, but that Patrick appealed to his father's best self and called it forth.

Another factor in this man's sobriety was the continuing, non-abandoning support he received from other recovering alcoholics in AA, where he, in turn, had a chance to help others. If you are dealing with a situation involving alcoholism and you are not a recovering alcoholic yourself, you might bring up the subject of Alcoholic Anonymous, which has a very high success rate, and also provides community as well as round-the-clock help.

Alcoholics may stay in denial for a long time, but it is important to have patience with their process. We hear a lot, these days, about being codependent, about being "enablers" of people with "problems" by sympathizing with them, rather than urging them to initiate change. It is sometimes suggested that we withdraw our support and relationship as a way to motivate people to make huge, life-changing decisions, and take tremendous steps into the unknown. It is my belief that such steps and changes cannot be made in a twinkling, nor should they be. It is also my belief that it is an unfair form of emotional blackmail to use your relationship with someone as a prize to be given or yanked away, depending on how cooperative another person may be with what you see as best for them.

We often practice this reward /punishment form of motivation with small children, and, quite often, adults react with subconscious echoes of such experiences in their own childhood. Sometimes, I think that the specter of co-dependency can occasionally be used as a way out for us, when we are exasperated or tired or angry. It is difficult to seek a balance between reinforcing a problem and reinforcing the person.

Here, again, we must distinguish between the person and his or her difficulty. There is a familiar saying that offers much wisdom: "Hate the sin; love the sinner." The person is not his or her problem. I do not think we should ever withdraw our emotional support from a person we companion, although we may be frank about his or her struggle, whatever that may be.

I have a close friend who is accomplished, compassionate, steady, and gifted. She is a devoted friend to others, a generous spirit, and a highly responsible artist who always meets her deadlines. There was one area in her life where there was, as another friend termed it, "something out of sync:" her marriage. It was a troubled marriage, but a complex one: nothing was outrageously wrong, but many things, including communication and emotional intimacy, were not at all right.

The marriage was a conundrum to my friend, a long-running theme that began to take on a certain circularity: a separation, a reconciliation, another separation, yet another reconciliation, a time of great separateness within the marriage.

People gave her advice: told her to leave; told her to stay. After awhile, for fear of burdening her friends, this woman struggled silently with her marriage. Even with the help of long-term counseling, she could not seem to find the answer for many years, until, at last, she knew she had done all she could, and finally felt she could break this attachment. She told me how deeply she appreciated all the friends who stuck with her and loved her as the good person she was, never judging her by this struggle.

She also remembers one friend who told her she could not continue their relationship because it was "enabling the problem." Ten years later, these words still stung. My friend has kept all the cards written to her over the years thanking her for her friendship and saying, "I am always here." But she also remembers this one friend with whom she had shared Masses and retreats, who turned on her in judgment. What finally helped her to make this tremendous life-change"The steady love of those who stuck by me, and called forth my best and strongest self with their belief in me," she said. Our steady presence with a person in difficulty can *enable* that best self and call it forth — even call it into action. Healing, on a deep level, begins when the person is put in touch with his or her power. I believe that we can truly harm people by conditional caring and the threat of abandonment.

On the other hand, there may be times when we need a dignified pull back, a withdrawal behind our lines of defense. Burnout can sneak up on us. It is a possibility that all caregivers must face, sooner or later.

Burnout

"How do you know when you've done enough?"

"How much is enough?"

"Am I giving too much? Too little?"

"I'm exhausted, but I can't let him down."

"I'm starting to feel I'm doing everything wrong."

"My fuse is really short lately."

"Why doesn't anybody else give a damn?"

These are common cries for help when a caregiver begins to experience burnout. Some consider burnout unavoidable in the helping professions, but I disagree. I think there are certain steps we can take to minimize or avoid burnout before it sneaks up on us.

First, look for warning signs in yourself and danger signals in the other person. If you start to dread a visit, if you start to feel drained, pay attention. Your psyche is telling you something. If the person you companion seems to be sliding into deeper difficulty, and you have not made a referral, now is the time. A heightened sense of awareness of your process, as well as your companion's, is the first step.

Next, spread the support network as wide as you can without overwhelming the person in need. Sometimes we want to do it all, and we think we should be able to be super saint. It is a humbling experience to realize that we quite often cannot. On the other hand, there is great joy in working with other people as a kind of helping team.

I will never forget the camaraderie and humor among the members of my chaplain team at Sibley Hospital; the cafeteria lunches laced with lemonade and black humor as we listened with one ear to the overhead pager for the next Code Blue. And I will never forget that same spirit of humorous camaraderie in shelter kitchens and nursing home hallways.

Community in crisis is a powerful thing and although you give up the chance to be a martyred saint, you gain a new sense of holy ground in the company of other helpers. When a close friend of mine, mentioned elsewhere in this book, lay dying of AIDS, all his friends formed a kind of unspoken rotation and each contributed something different. No one person could have practiced the art of caring alone in that situation. At the same time, numbers did not negate each individual's contributions.

One person arranged for visits from "Food and Friends," a group like Meals-on-Wheels; another person sent flowers every week; one took care of weekly laundry; others rotated as visitors. Others brought a favorite sorbet from a gourmet grocery store. Another dropped a book or magazine by. Together the weave was multi-stranded and rich, an example of caregiving as an ensemble company.

Such ensembles take many forms. In Chapter Three, I referred to the eviction of an indigent woman on a cold January night. It was I who sat there on the street with this woman and shared dinner with her, until she could bring herself to go with me to a shelter. But I was only one of a network which helped this woman put her shattered life together to form a new picture: the shelter providers, social workers, a parish willing to store the woman's belongings, and other homeless women. All helped Jenny begin her life again in a halfway house with her trunk of favorite books, and enough money from Social Security and a disability service to enable her to move about the city she so enjoyed.

There is a certain satisfaction in working with others in the art of caring because, somehow, as everyone works together, we offer caring to one another, as well. The very act itself seems to call forth this grace, this gift. Jesus said, "The kingdom of heaven is like a net that was thrown into the sea and caught fish of every kind; which when it was full, they drew it ashore...." (Matthew 14:47-48a).

When we share the art of caring, we not only guard against individual burnout, but I also believe we may catch a glimpse of the reign of God, as we all pull in those nets that take in so many forms.

Practitioners of the art of caring may sometimes feel guilty about taking a break. But the most effective caregivers I have known understand their own rhythms and use them. In the famous words of Ecclesiastes (3:1), "For everything there is a season, and a time for every matter under heaven." We cannot expect our interior orchard to be in constant harvest time. Nor should we demand that the caregiving impulse be in full, glorious bloom like the magnolia and cherry blossoms bursting all over Washington, D.C., as I write. There are times, as wise Carmelite nun told me long ago, of "winter growth," when everything that happens in the garden occurs under the soil, invisible but present.

If we are to sustain the art of caring as a lifestyle, we need to know our own seasons and rhythms. There are certain times of day when we are strongest and have the most energy. There are certain internal seasons, too, in which we are hardier or more prone to tire.

Each caregiving process also has its own rhythms and seasons because this is a living, growing process. It has its new and full moons, its growing and dormant seasons. And so do we. There are times when we may need to push against the desire to remain dormant; when we may use reluctance or fatigue as a cover-up for fear of involvement, intimacy, or challenge. There are also times when we need to seek spiritual and physical refreshment. If we factor these experiences into our expectations, we can make them a part of our routine, instead of seeing them as failures or allowing them to turn into canceled appointments or absent gazes, which may be interpreted as abandonment or rejection.

I think it is important to allow a certain amount of time each week and each month for a "quiet day" or "quiet morning" in which we turn off the phone, or walk in a park alone, or sit in a church, or by a lake, or in front of a beloved painting in a museum. We may use such "quiet times" for prayer and reflection and also quite simply for rest and respite.

Silent retreats now and then are also spiritually nourishing for me and for many people (although they are not for everyone). You may prefer a directed retreat or one with a special focus, such as healing. The important thing is to find the form of spiritual refreshment that nourishes you, whatever it is.

A different refreshment comes from companionship. Many people who practice the art of caring have trusted prayer partners with whom they share needs, concerns, feelings of exhaustion, and intercessory prayer. For several years, I have had two prayer partners, each in a different city. Because we know each other so well, we can close our eyes, pray on the phone, and through the power of the Holy Spirit feel we are in the same room. In a way, we are.

I also find it helpful to have access to prayerful communities to support me in the art of caring and to support my intercessions and those I companion. For a long time,

I have been close to a Carmelite monastery on the opposite coast from mine, which I visit as often as I can and with which I am often in communication. Over the years, these Carmelites have prayed as a community for many intentions I have brought them, and have prayed support and intercession for people in my circle of concern.

There are many such communities whose vocation is prayer. It might be helpful to make a list of three or four. It is very comforting to go to bed with the knowledge that someone in Carmel is sitting in the chapel and praying for someone who needs prayer as desperately as you need your sleep.

Caregivers also need some boundaries. We hear a lot about "boundary issues" today — respecting others emotional boundaries and discerning where our own begin and end. As with many psychosocial terms, I have mixed feelings about this designation. On one hand, I sometimes feel suspicious of an overemphasis on "boundary issues," people insisting on "their space" above all, and I find myself wondering if these terms are simply euphemistic ways to say, "I don't want to get involved / take the time / get too close."

Certainly, that was what a friend's fiancé meant when he used both of those phrases in one sentence. That is a relational example, but I have heard it extended into the art of caring. I recall a conversation with a couple from a part of the country where self-reliance is given high priority. This couple refused to reach out to anyone beyond family and one close friend. Their philosophy was that any broader spectrum of caring *inevitably* crossed boundary lines and, besides, reinforced the "weakness" of such groups as the homeless, who "should stand on their own two feet anyway."

Nevertheless, I do believe that certain psychological boundary lines are important to recognize. We need to know where our psyches begin and end in order to avoid the mistaken notion that we are merged with someone else. Empathetic people can sometimes identify so strongly with others that these distinctions become blurred. Usually we can be more helpful to others when we remain empathetic, yet retain a sense of perspective about who we are and what our limits are as well.

It is sometimes important to set boundaries on phone conversations and the length of visits, as well as our availability. This is not to be stingy, but to avoid creating a sense of dependency in the other person. This only robs that person of his or her own inherent power to heal and regain control of a situation or life itself. (The creation of wider support networks also mitigates against dependent relationships.)

One of my most respected mentors, Sr. Mary Ann Luby, who directed Rachel's Shelter for Homeless Women, understood the business of boundaries very well and balanced it with her warm accessibility. She knew all about burnout and guarded against it by choosing to live in an apartment with a roommate in a different neighborhood from the shelter. At the end of the day, she could retreat to her home, cook and listen to music, read and talk with her friend. This oasis in her daily routine enabled her to direct a busy, downtown shelter for over a decade.

By contrast, some other shelter providers I have known chose to live in the shelters themselves. Most of these caregivers moved on after about a year. I think that Sister Mary Ann Luby's rhythm is an important lesson to us in pacing ourselves as we practice the art of caring.

Other important examples present themselves. A priest I know who specializes in pastoral care takes one day off a month to attend to what he calls *sarx* needs. *Sarx* is the Greek word for "flesh," as opposed to *pneuma,* the spirit. Although this priest certainly recognizes the need for spiritual refreshment, he feels that *sarx* is often neglected by caregivers, and perhaps deemed inferior to the spiritual.

As the New Testament reminds us, we are "earthen vessels." And as Christians, we have an incarnational spirituality. The part of us that constitutes *sarx* needs attention, and should not be dichotomized from the spiritual but should be integrated with it. Thus, the priest takes a day to work out at a gym, have a steam bath, and a good meal with a glass of wine. This sort of refreshment, he believes, should not be out of bounds; it forms another kind of retreat experience.

Exercise of all kinds is helpful in relieving stress and quite often caregivers find solutions to problems as they jog, or walk, or work out. Or perhaps no solutions appear at all. Just as well. The point of exercise is maintaining a healthy balance between the spiritual and physical poles of our being and nurturing *both* so that we may maintain the strength to nurture others.

Often overlooked is the form of nurture that comes through the arts. Earlier we discussed using the arts in the practice of the art of caring. So many people respond to one or another of the arts in a way that deeply touches the emotions; the arts, therefore, can be used very powerfully as we companion people in difficulty. But why should we overlook the power of the arts when it comes to sustaining the caregiver within each of us?

Perhaps it is music that refreshes you; perhaps it is settling into a room in a favorite museum to drink in the beauty of some beloved paintings. Perhaps you have always found solace and rejuvenation from poetry or literature, the movies, theater, or the dance. If you haven't, you might try some of these areas and allow the arts to speak to your soul. A very caring friend of mine says she could not live without music.

I have often wondered if this friend could have so much patience with other people and so many original ideas as a caregiver, if she did not have the vast ocean of music to swim in whenever she needs refreshment.

Then, again, you may be someone who paints or draws or writes or sings or works with clay. As you increase and expand the practice of caring, you may find that the practice of these other arts become more important for you, as outlets and as expressions of all the new discoveries you make as you companion others.

Learning how best to refresh yourself is crucial to preventing burnout before it happens. In the Gospel of Mark, early on, we catch a glimpse of Jesus' first full day of his Galilean ministry. He healed the sick, and he performed exorcisms. "At sundown, they brought to him all who were sick or possessed with demons. And the whole city was gathered around the door. And he cured many who were sick ... and cast out many demons.... In the morning, while it was still very dark, he got up and went out to a deserted place, and there he prayed" (Mark 1:3235).

Jesus himself gives us an example of how we might pace ourselves in the art of caring. Throughout the gospels Jesus "missed lunch" as a priest friend once remarked, so busy was he with his ministry. Throughout the gospels, as well, Jesus retreated to pray alone. This rhythm seems a kind of holy dance between community and solitude, between active and reflective caring.

It is a dance that we can all learn; perhaps it is a dance we were born knowing and somehow have forgotten. If we wish to learn it again, its steps are ours and the Dance-master awaits us with open arms.

■

<9>

The Rewards of Caring

For I am convinced that neither death, nor life, nor angels, nor rulers, nor things present, nor things to come, nor powers, nor height, nor depth, nor anything else in all creation, will be able to separate us from the love of God in Christ Jesus, our Lord.

—Romans 8:38-39

She stood in the dingy hallway of a shelter and pointed to the water-stained wall. The light came in thin and gray, slanting across her cracked glasses. She pushed her dust-colored hair away from her face; a face curiously childlike for a sixty-year-old woman. On the wall was a drawing she had done of a clock. The time read 5:07. The drawing was a good one, and I told her so; she had dated it months before and, oddly enough, the date happened to be my birthday. As I told her this, her face seemed illuminated from within. Lifting her chin, she began to sing in a slow, stately, sacred way — the way a soprano sings the national anthem, perhaps.

The song she sang was "Happy Birthday." It did not matter that this was not my birthday. In many ways, it was hers; it was ours. Later, when I reported this seemingly "small" event to the nun who ran the shelter, she nodded, at first as if to herself. "That's the best reward you could get," my wise mentor said. "She got to give you something. Mostly, the women here, they don't get that chance — the chance to give anything to anyone. To give someone the chance *to give* is a gift in itself. Best kind."

It is eight years since Nora sang "Happy Birthday" to me. In a dim hall, on the "wrong" day. And, yet, I remember it. I remember it on many days and nights and weeks and know I always will. Such moments of grace, communion, and connection are among the greatest rewards, for me, of practicing the art of caring.

There are other moments: exhaustion, burnout, and "I've had it, I don't need this" moments. There are times when no one thanks you, when no one looks up, when no one seems to notice or care what you do. There are times when what you have to give seems so small as to be totally useless and insignificant.

It is important to expect such moments and see them as a part of that endless weave of color and texture, of voice and gesture and life-crossing-life that you begin when you practice the art of caring. Mentors have told me that caregiving burnout is common, precisely because people expect to *get a high* from the act itself.

Sr. Mary Ann, a holy nun and shelter director becomes impatient just before Thanksgiving, when the shelter phone rings incessantly with callers wanting to serve turkey on the holiday. When told that regular volunteers served on Thanksgiving, the callers were inevitably disappointed. Could they come back in January she would ask. For some reason, no one ever could.

My friend, this dedicated nun in blue jeans, would come away muttering from the phone. "I wonder," she would ask the air, "do they want to feel good about themselves? Or make these women feel good?" Time and time again, she said people burned out because their expectations were unrealistic, and I can tell you from my own experience that if you practice the art of caring only to feel good about yourself, you will be disappointed.

Sometimes you will leave a situation and think of all the things you could have done, should have done, did not do. Other times you'll come away wondering if this is any of your business. Why get involved? Your own life is complicated enough. Sometimes you'll be out of patience, out of gas. But as in all vocations and all committed relationships, if you choose to practice the art of caring, for the long haul, the big picture, the now-and forever, you will learn to flex with the up-and-down rhythms that are inevitable. You don't judge a necklace by one bead.

For me, the rewards of caring come in several forms. One of the most important is the reward of the witness. That's what I was when Nora sang to me in the hallway. I did very little. I felt awed and privileged to witness her self-expression, her transcendence of brokenness, and her newly claimed ability to be the giver and the gift. That's what it was the day I stood in a prayer circle with a group of suffering women and lifted my head as I heard then spontaneously begin to sing, "We Shall Overcome."

I was a witness that time a depressed man baked a pan of brownies, and I was a witness when a seriously depressed, divorced woman picked out a new dress with a bright yolk-yellow top. If you think through your life, you, too, have been a witness to those moments of grace when, perhaps for just a moment, someone else's life brushes yours and there is a crackle of connection, and where you stand, in that moment, is abruptly holy ground. When you practice the art of caring, you come to witness more small miracles than you have ever seen before — and they stay with you.

We live in a deracinated, disconnected society. More and more now, as the Baby Boomers move into their fifties, people want to see beyond the usual concepts of success. In what Gail Sheehy calls "Second Adulthood," we find ourselves open to the possibility of witnessing miracles, large and small.

What does that mean for you?

Perhaps it means a smile breaking across a depressed neighbor's face. Perhaps it means the grip of a hand from a hospital bed, or a moment when your eyes meet a colleague's eyes as the two of you together clean out a soon-to-be-vacated office. When you stand with others, at those liminal places, those threshold places, you share a sense of connection that rarely comes in our time, our world.

We witness legal documents; we witness marriage bands and treaties. These small moments of caring are surely just as important. The role of witness seems to me a special one and a humbling one; we are allowed to glimpse through the windows of the soul.

Another reward in the art of caring seems more obvious. It comes in the form of the homemade cross of nails, made for me by a hospital patient — a cross that hangs on our front door. It comes in the form of a note of gratitude, a dried flower presented as a token of thanks. These rewards are very precious, and were the house to burn, I would reach for those ahead of most things.

I remember the butcher who came every Thursday when I was a child, to leave a special delicacy (often, brains) for my father, a surgeon, who would not charge this man who could not pay. It didn't really matter what the butcher left in his carefully folded brown paper bag; what mattered was what he left unsaid every Thursday at ten in the morning. And what mattered, too, was his dignity, which was never taken from him.

I remember other gifts from my father's grateful patients. But I believe, for my father, as well as for me, there were and are greater ones. In his case, there were lives saved. In my case, there were those moments when differences melted away and human beings were in solidarity, were one.

Once you begin to experience these miracles, you experience even more. As Andrew Weil, M.D., writes,

> Years ago I met a woman who was able to find four-leaf clovers in any clover patch. She liked to bet people that within any minute ... she could find a four-leaf clover. And she always won the bets. Never having found one, I was completely mystified ... but after meeting this woman and watching her do it, something changed for me. I realized the key to her success was her belief that in any clover patch there was a four-leaf clover to be found. With/ that belief, there is a chance of finding it; without it, there is none. After meeting her, I began to look again and soon I started to find four-*leaf* clovers (Spontaneous Healing).

We live in an age where we want to make a difference And many of us are reaching a place in our lives where that seems increasingly important on a spiritual level. On March 27, 1996, in the *Washington Post,* an article ran dead center on the front page: "Sometimes Money Isn't Enough." The subhead was "Searching for More, Careerists Opt for Making a Difference Over Making a Bundle."

The article cited various people in Washington, DC's fast lane who opted for a different way of life. Reporter Sandra Evans wrote about a successful woman who, "not long ago was a top professional at NBC News, working the 1992 presidential election, jetting to foreign hot spots with anchor Tom Brokaw, pulling down a six-figure salary. And wanting, so badly, to get out. Now she makes $31,000 a year at Martha's Table, an urban oasis for the needy.... Her longest journey these days is into their souls. And she loves it."

Philip Collyer, executive director of Greater DC Cares, said, "It's happening more and more ... It's related to the boomer generation hitting middle-age." The article goes on to note, "... a small army of people leaving traditional careers to look for spiritual growth. These people are looking for a truer meaning of their lives," says Gerald Celente, director of Capital Trends Research. "The core of it is a different type of spirituality.... We are living in very empty times. There is not a lot of inner joy or an outer exclamation of it."

LeAnn Gregory Boyd decided work at a computer software firm was not enough. "I was tired of the callousness and shallowness of the for-profit world.... It was not bringing out the best in me.... The raises kept coming and the promotions kept coming, but it was an empty well."

Now she works full-time at Central Union Mission. According to this and other recent articles, more and more people are looking for a new kind of meaning in their lives through the art of caring.

You may not be called to chuck your job and change your entire lifestyle. You may not be called to work with the financially poor, or the terminally ill. What matters is that you discover where you are called to practice the art of caring — as a witness to moments of grace, as one who empowers others, as one who makes a difference, as a miracle watcher and finder of four-leaf clovers.

I began my own journey into the art of caring without realizing it. About ten years ago, I began noticing homeless women, as if for the first time. I noticed, I watched, I thought and prayed about the homeless, but I did absolutely nothing different. Then one Advent, I abruptly decided to volunteer once a week in a shelter where I served dinner to homeless women. "Just for Advent," I told myself. That Advent lasted six years, until I felt called to another practice of the art of caring. Once you really look into other people's faces, it is difficult to look away again.

This book, however, is focused on the faces of your immediate circle, and they are no less worthy than those in shelters or prisons. The invisible poor are everywhere — and sometimes they are us. Among your friends, your neighbors, your coworkers, if you look, you will find opportunities to reach out to companion others through the shadowlands, to practice the ministry of presence and the art of caring as only you can. It is a very individual and creative art.

There are also reasons of faith that enable us to practice the art of caring and that, indeed, provide a mandate. Jesus washed his disciples' feet and gave a new commandment, "Love one another as I have loved you." In Matthew 25:32-40, a passage which inspired me at the beginning of my journey, Jesus addresses the blessed: "For I was hungry and you gave me food, I was thirsty and you gave me something to drink, I was a stranger and you welcomed me, I was naked and you gave me clothing, I was sick and you took care of me, I was in prison and you visited me." When, Jesus was asked, did we do these things? And he answered, "In as much as you have done it to the least of these my children you have done it to me."

I think it is a great mistake to imagine that the hungry, the thirsty, the stranger, and the naked, the sick, and the imprisoned must be "out there some place." Perhaps it is more comfortable for us to think so. Certain things, we are taught or choose to believe, do not happen to "people like us" — our neighbors, our coworkers, our friends, our families. And, yet, I believe that is precisely where we discover a great deal of the above conditions we never saw before.

Perhaps, as with the four-leaf clovers, we did not see them. Much of the time, I believe, we may see, but do not know what to do, how to do it, when or where, or which road will open out before us once we begin to act. It is said we live in empty times. In his own time, in 19th century New England, Henry David Thoreau wrote that most people live lives of quiet desperation.

It is those lives, those everyday car pool faces that we may touch through the art of caring — and in so doing, we may change our own lives of quiet desperation, lives filled with "if only's" and "might have been's." By practicing the art of caring, we participate in the gospel, we find four-leaf clovers, and we make those fragile, grace-filled connections that seem impossible to so many of us in our fast-lane, high-tech world. This world, once again, can be infused with a spiritual dimension, once the art of caring becomes a part of our lives.

In Edgar Lee Master's classic *Spoon River Anthology,* the author takes us for a walk through the graveyard of his small, Midwest hometown. There we read epitaphs as poems; poems which capture the essence of each life and distills it like a kind of amber. One voice speaks to me most clearly from this graveyard about the art of caring — defining it and showing what it can mean to us all; everyone of us.

Hear the voice of the fictitious Faith Matheny, a mystical Irish-American transplant to this Ohio town and you will hear the promise and the grace inherent in the caring art:

At first, you may not know what they mean, And you
*   may never know,*
And we may never tell you:

These sudden flashes in your soul,
Like lambent lightning on snowy clouds
At midnight when the moon is full.
They come in solitude, or perhaps
You sit with your friend, and all at once
A silence falls on speech, and his eyes
Without a flicker glow at you: —
You too have seen the secret together,
He sees it in you, and you in him.
And there you sit thrilling lest the Mystery
Stand before you and strike you dead
With a splendor like the sun's.
Be brave, all souls who have such visions!
As your body's alive as mine is dead,
You're catching a little whiff of the ether
Reserved for God Himself.

■

Reading and Reference List

Benatovich, Beth, *What We Know So Far: Wisdom Among Women.* New York: St. Martin's Press, 1991.

Clinebell, Howard John, *Mental Health Through Christian Community; The Local Church's Ministry of Growth and Healing.* New York: Abingdon Press, 1965.

————*Counseling for Spiritually Empowered Wholeness; A Hope-Centered Approach.* New York: Haworth Pastoral Press, 1995.

————*Basic Types of Pastoral Care and Counseling: Resources for the Ministry of Healing and Growth.* Nashville: Abingdon Press, 1984.

Curry, Cathleen, *When Your Parent Dies.* Notre Dame, IN: Ave Maria Press, 1993.

————, *When Your Spouse Dies.* Notre Dame, IN: Ave Maria Press, 1990.

Dass, Ram and Gorman, Paul, *How Can I Help?: Stories and Reflections on Service.* New York: Alfred A. Knopf, 1985.

Friedman, Edwin H., *Generation to Generation: Family Process in Church and Synagogue.* New York: Guilford Press, 1985.

Greteman, James and Joseph Dunne, *When Divorce Happens.* Notre Dame, IN: Ave Maria Press, 1990.

Kubler-Ross, Elisabeth, AIDS: *The Ultimate Challenge.* New York: Collier Books,1993.
————, *On Death and Dying.* New York: Collier Books, 1993.

Martz, Sandra Haldeman, ed., *When I Am an Old Woman I Shall Wear Purple.* Watsonville, CA: Papier-Mache, 1991.

MacNutt, Francis, *Healing.* Notre Dame, IN: Ave Maria Press, 1974.
————, *The Power to Heal.* Notre Dame, IN: Ave Maria Press, 1977.
————, *The Prayer That Heals.* Notre Dame, IN: Ave Maria Press, 1981.

Nuland, Sherwin B., *How We Die: Reflections On Life's Final Chapter.* New York, Random House, 1994.

Pregent, Carol, *When a Child Dies.* Notre Dame, IN: Ave Maria Press, 1992.

Rupp, Joyce, *Praying Our Goodbyes.* Notre Dame, IN: Ave Maria Press, 1988.

Stoddard, Alexandra, *Making Choices. The Joy of a Courageous Life.* New York, William Morrow & Co. Inc., 1994.

Thomas, Leo & Jan Alkire, *Healing as a Parish Ministry.* Notre Dame, IN: Ave Maria Press, 1992.

Westberg, Granger E., *Good Grief A Constructive Approach to the Problem of Loss.* Rock Island, IL: Augustana Press, 1962.

Wicks, Robert J. and Robert M. Hamma, *A Circle of Friends.* Notre Dame, IN: Ave Maria Press, 1996.

Wolff, Pierre, *May I Hate God,* New York: Paulist Press, 1979.

Critical acclaim for other works by Marcy Heidish
Novels:

- *A Woman Called Moses*, Houghton Mifflin Co.
    - The acclaimed historical novel based on the amazing life of Harriet Tubman, legendary conductor on the Underground Railroad.
    - A Literary Guild Alternate Selection
    - A TV Movie, starring Cicely Tyson.

Praise for *A Woman Called Moses:*

• *Publishers Weekly*: [Harriet Tubman's] "story has been told before, but never as eloquently, almost poetically, as here...achingly real...a strong narrative of a totally committed woman, one who speaks directly to our own desperate need to feel committed — and our wish that somewhere in the world there were more people like Harriet Tubman."

• *The Washington Post Book World*: "Profoundly rewarding...a daring work of the imagination."

• *Chicago Sun Times*: "Marcy Heidish has, almost uncannily, crawled into the skin and very mind of Harriet Tubman....The dialogue sings with poetic beauty."

- *Witnesses*, Houghton Mifflin Co.
    - Historical novel based on the life of lay minister Anne Hutchinson, religious freedom advocate.

Praise for *Witnesses:*

• *The New York Times Book Review:* "....nothing ordinary about her creation of this remarkable woman. The novel abounds in literary grace, employing the voices of the times as though heard this minute."

• *The New Yorker Magazine*: "A striking novel...a compelling portrait."

• *The Washington Post*: "Pure pleasure. Anne Hutchinson is real; thanks to *Witnesses,* she at last assumes her proper place...in American history." —Jonathan Yardley, Pulitzer Prize-winning critic.

■ *The Torching*, Simon & Schuster.
   -Contemporary literary novel, hardcover and paper-back.
   -Literary Guild Alternate Selection; laudatory reviews.

Praise for <u>The Torching</u>:

• ***Washington Post Book World***: "Flex your fingers, gentle readers. You're going to be turning pages for the next few hours.... Because of Heidish's skill, we get the full force of her double-whammy...in part due to the grace with which she weaves the present-day and the historical, but also because of her inventiveness at the book's close, the daring way she gets both strands of plot to unite.... Marcy Heidish is a stylish and intelligent novelist to boot, more than up to the dizzying, tale-spinning task that she set for herself here."

• ***Kirkus Reviews:*** "Shuddery mystery-suspense with supernatural overtones."

• ***Library Journal:*** "Intricately constructed...A deliciously spine-tingling, multi-layered literary mystery..."

• ***Publishers Weekly***: "Subtle and gratifying psychological suspense...Penetrating characterizations...Heidish impeccably orchestrates the historical and contemporary, the supernatural and psychological."

•***Simon & Schuster:*** With this spellbinding tale of mysticism, horror, and history, a gifted, award-winning writer ... here gives us a novel to rival the works of Anne Rice, Alfred Hitchcock, or Edgar Allan Poe — a vivid tale of an eighteenth-century midwife ... sentenced to burn as a witch in the tiny town of Maidstone, Maryland.... *The Torching* is an unforgettable novel about the power of words..."

■ *A Dangerous Woman: Mother Jones, An Unsung American Heroine*, Dolan & Associates, Publishers.
   - an outstanding novel of a self-proclaimed Hell Raiser.

■ *Miracles*, New American Library.

- Historical novel based on the life of Mother Elizabeth Seton, first American-born canonized saint.

Praise for *Miracles*:

• *New American Library*: *Miracles* is a novel charged with the vitality of a life that saw many changes, and with the power of a love that took many forms...as a lonely daughter of a wealthy, indifferent man; a searching young woman; a contented matron embracing a marriage that produced five beloved children; a widow searching for new meaning to life.

• *The New York Times Book Review*: This appealing book, told from the point of view of a skep-tical modern priest, moves swiftly through tragedy to triumph.

• *Kirkus Reviews:* Working delicately with a balance of Church hagiography and psychological insight, Heidish provides another strong focus on the root dilemma of female saints and achievers.

■ *The Secret Annie Oakley*, New American Library.

- Historical novel based on the life of the legendary sharpshooter.

Praise for *The Secret Annie Oakley:*

• *Kirkus Reviews*: "An immensely touching and cohesive fictional biography of the legendary sharp-shooter... builds from exemplary research to a fresh portrait of a talented woman in crisis...a class act —as Heidish reconstructs. with color and drama, the choreography of the shows, the tone of the period, and the textures of a haunting past."

• *The Arizona Daily Star*: "Marcy Heidish is an imaginative, amazing writer. She's a magician with words.... Each character has been brought to life with a mere pen stroke; flesh and blood beings that are more than fiction.... A masterpiece of creative writing."

• *The Kansas City Star:* "An unforgettable story."

- **Deadline**, St. Martin's Press.
  - Contemporary psychological novel with a "mystery" as a narrative line.
  - Nominee for prestigious national "Edgar" Award; fine reviews.

<u>Praise for *Deadline*</u>:

• **Washington Post**: "*Deadline* is a tense, well-turned tale, filled with authentic police and newspaper people. Heidish's taut, punchy style moves the story at lightning speed."

• **Kirkus Reviews**: "The high-tension plot is enhanced by sharply etched pictures, by many vivid characters, and by a crisp, clean, first-person style. Heidish imbues her haunting story and her gutsy heroine with a rare sense of tenderness and poignancy. An impressive mystery by a gifted writer."

• **St. Martin's Press:** "This wire-tight novel probes relentlessly, driving deep into psychological darkness and violent death. As the riveting story reaches its stunning conclusion, we see a complex woman forced to meet the ultimate deadline."

Non-Fiction Books:

- **A Candle At Midnight**, Ave Maria Press.

<u>Praise for *A Candle At Midnight*</u>:

• "...fills a void in popular literature about depression. ...She recognizes that making one's way through the agony and terror of depression is a spiritual pilgrimage as well. She has constructed a meaningful collection of readings, rituals, and suggestions that have great practical utility. I recommend this book to anyone." – Martha M. Manning, Author of *Undercurrents: A Life Beneath the Surface*.

• "Heidish honors modern medicine and spiritual healing in this compelling work." – Alen J. Salerian, M.D., Medical Director of the Washington Psychiatric Center.

• "A masterpiece!" – Rev. Nancy Eggert, Director of the Shalem Center for Spiritual Direction.

■ *Soul and the City*, WaterBrook Press, Random House imprint.

<u>Praise for *Soul and the City*</u>:

• "I actually started reading Marcy Heidish's *Soul and the City* on a subway train, and I must say it had exactly the effect she writes about. It gave me peace in the middle of the hurry, the rush, the loud noise of the city." – Rick Hamlin, executive editor of *Guideposts* and author of *Finding God on the A Train*.

• "... a rich and nuanced touring companion to rival any Michelin or Eyewitness guide—usable in any city of the world. Keep it close and...you will meet beauty and holiness no matter where you pause to look." – Leigh McLeroy, author of *The Beautiful Ache* and *The Sacred Ordinary*.

■ *Defiant Daughters: Christian Women of Conscience*, Liguori Publications.

<u>Praise for *Defiant Daughters*</u>:

• *Liguori Publications*: Joan of Arc, Immaculée Ilibagiza, Corrie ten Book, and Sojourner Truth are among those women whom best-selling author Marcy Heidish calls "Defiant Daughters."

This informative, challenging, and entertaining book spotlights the lives of more than 20 spiritual trailblazers and their responses to crises of conscience. They represent different races, denominations, and nations, but all are feisty — often fiery — and always faithful to their callings.

What motivated these "defiant daughters," who gave their all for God? Heidish seeks out the decisive juncture where they took a stand for conscience, regardless of the consequences. This stunning and compelling book will bring you face-to-face with an unforgettable female gallery of "profiles in courage."

■ *Who Cares? Simple Ways YOU Can Reach Out*, Ave Maria Press.

An ideal resource for anyone interested in engaged spirituality.

This practical book is designed to bring out the caring person in each of us. Heidish offers simple, specific ways to practice the art of caring, especially within our immediate circle of concern.

Praise for *Who Cares?*:

· *Cultural Information Service:* "Contains savvy insights and wisdom about service... This is an ideal resource for anyone interested in engaged spirituality."

· *Fredericksburg Free Lance-Star*: "Covers just about every topic imaginable on ways that people can reach out to one another ... [written] in an easy-to-follow simple-style prose."

Short Pieces:

· Articles and book reviews published in *Ms.* Magazine, *GEO* Magazine, *The Washington Post*, *The Washington Star*, and various in-flight periodicals.

· "*The Pilgrim Who Stayed*," *GEO* Magazine, about Chartres Cathedral, widely translated into many languages.

· "*The Grand Dame of the Harbor*," about the Statue of Liberty, a highly acclaimed cover story for *GEO* Magazine.

This article is included in a textbook anthology designed to teach writing to college students.

www.ingramcontent.com/pod-product-compliance
Lightning Source LLC
Chambersburg PA
CBHW070955040426
42443CB00007B/519